Praise for *Down[...]*

As a fitness and wellness expert, I've coached numerous clients that have had to deal with the devastating effects of rejection . . . mentally, physically, and spiritually. Tracey brilliantly taps into the deeper meanings of rejection and how to leverage the experiences to your advantage. *Downside Up* is not only a catchy title, but an invaluable tool that I will be sharing with all my clients. Thank you, Tracey, for your wisdom and insight.

Wendie Pett, fitness and wellness expert; TV show host

Divas, drama queens, green-eyed monsters, fudge, and fairy tales—*Downside Up* has them all! More important, it has everything you need to learn how to use rejection as a stepping-stone to personal confidence and power. Tracey Mitchell has lived through excruciating rejection and transformed it into a life of international Christian influence, hope, and joy. Practical. Poignant. And positive. You can't help but benefit from this excellent book. Read it and reap!

Mary Hollingsworth, best-selling author,
***Hugs for Women* and many others**

Tracey Mitchell has diligently and conscientiously written this compelling book to help anyone who has experienced emotional distress and desires to step out of bondage into God's maximum potential and fulfillment in life. Tracey's simple approach helps the reader feel confident in releasing the abilities and purpose God has placed within them. Don't miss this opportunity to experience restoration from everything the enemy has meant for your defeat.

Dr. Iris Delgado, founder, Crowned With Purpose; best-selling author, *Satan, You Can't Have My Children*

Dr. Mitchell has been gifted by the Lord to communicate a clear and effective message of hope to a hurting world. Through a well-balanced approach of wisdom and the personal experiences, *Downside Up* will guide its readers on the journey from brokenness to wellness. I highly recommend *Downside Up* for anyone who suffers from the pain and scars of rejection.

Pastor Asa Dockery, senior pastor, World Harvest Church North; author; television host

The sound-bite sections of wisdom in *Downside Up* are captivating, clever, and utterly compelling. In a world where the pain of rejection hovers like a toxic fog, Tracey Mitchell's insight, perception, and sense of humor is a breath of fresh air.

Allison Bottke, author, the Setting Boundaries * **series, including** *Setting Boundaries with Your Adult Children*; **editor,** *God Allows U-Turns* **anthology**

Tracey's writing is like her life—real, authentic, and transparent. She has a gift for communicating, especially to women, that is much needed. We live in a hurting world, and things are not getting any better. As Christians, our lives are not supposed to fall apart, but they do. In *Downside Up*, Tracey guides the reader on his or her journey from brokenness to wholeness. Often using personal examples, anyone who has felt the pain of personal rejection will be blessed by *Downside Up*. It's a must read for Christians who have been used, abused, and discarded.

Jack Watts, award-winning author, *Hi, My Name Is Jack, Recovering from Religious Abuse: 11 Steps to Spiritual Freedom, Real Prayers for Real People with Real Problems*, **and** *We Believe: 30 Days to Understanding our Heritage*; **creator, Pushing Jesus blog**

This book is a must-read for anyone who has gone through rejection, is going through it now, or will go through it in the future.

Suellen Roberts, founder and president, Christian Women in Media Association

In her new book, *Downside Up*, Tracey Mitchell states: "Society has distorted the truth about deception." Who would know this better than Tracey? This woman of uncommon faith writes with the passion and insight of one who has experienced rejection. Tracey understands brokenness and rejection. Rather than become overcome by hurts, however, she became the overcomer. As you read this book, let God touch your heart and turn your life *Downside Up*. Get ready for a transformation . . . in your life and in your world. Total victory is near!

J. Don George, DD, senior pastor, Calvary Church, Irving, Texas; author, *Against the Wind*

Downside Up offers a fresh, new look at an age-old issue that men and women deal with on a regular basis. Dr Tracey Mitchell gives solid advice while sharing her life experiences. Tracey asks thought-provoking questions while offering anecdotal evidence to back up her conclusions. Savvy, insightful, and inspiring: this is one of those books you just cannot put down.

Robin Bertram, national regions director, Christian Women in Media; executive producer, Freedom Today Television

Downside Up

Downside Up

TRANSFORM REJECTION
INTO YOUR
Golden Opportunity

Tracey Mitchell

THOMAS NELSON
Since 1798

NASHVILLE DALLAS MEXICO CITY RIO DE JANEIRO

Published in Nashville, Tennessee, by Thomas Nelson. Thomas Nelson is a registered trademark of Thomas Nelson, Inc.

Thomas Nelson, Inc., titles may be purchased in bulk for educational, business, fund-raising, or sales promotional use. For information, please e-mail SpecialMarkets@ThomasNelson.com.

Library of Congress Cataloging-in-Publication Data

Mitchell, Tracey, 1970–
  Downside up : transform rejection into your golden opportunity / Tracey Mitchell.
    pages cm
  Includes bibliographical references.
  ISBN 978-1-4002-0484-7
  1. Rejection (Psychology)—Religious aspects—Christianity. I. Title.
  BV4905.3.M57 2013
  248.8'6—dc23   2012045234

Printed in the United States of America

13 14 15 16 17 RRD 6 5 4 3 2 1

For Robby, my best friend and partner in life

Contents

Introduction   xiii

1. Rejection: Life's Golden Opportunity   1
2. Conquering the Need to Be Perfect   17
3. If You Love Me, Don't Leave Me   35
4. Divas, Deceivers, and Drama Queens   52
5. Green-Eyed Monsters   72
6. Families and Fudge   90
7. Truth, Lies, and Fairy Tales   111
8. Beautiful Distortions   129
9. Build Confidence; Laugh at Fear   147
10. The New You   165
11. Wave Good-bye to Your Past   182

Conclusion   195

Notes   199

Acknowledgments   201

About the Author   203

Introduction

I remember having lunch with a strikingly beautiful young woman. Talented and articulate, she had the potential to become whatever she desired. With tears dripping down her face she asked, "Tracey, why do I continue to chase after men who do not want me? What is wrong with me? I ignore those who accept me and pursue those who will not accept me." That, my dear friend, is the question of the ages: why do we continue to pursue things or people who are unwilling to pursue us? Why do we seek affirmation from those who are incapable of giving it?

In my travels around the world, I have experienced the extraordinary pleasure of meeting men and women from almost every walk of life. What continues to amaze me is not the cultural differences that divide us but rather the common thread of heartache uniting us. More than ever, I can attest that pain does not discriminate. I have watched the young, old, rich, poor, successful, attractive, and educated alike forsake their dreams because someone labeled them as unqualified or inferior.

Society has distorted the truth about rejection, and we have been solidly deceived. Most of us understand the negative aspects of rejection—the parts that thrive on our insecurities, bet against our potential, and uproot any seed of encouragement we can muster. But few of us have been taught how to embrace the positive aspects of rejection.

Everyone encounters rejection. The question is not whether rejection will happen but how you will respond when rejection strikes next. Will it develop, or destroy, your dream? Will it empower, or deflate, your confidence? How will you handle the next episode of rejection? Will you wilt beneath the fire of hurtful words, or will you use rejection as a springboard of opportunity to create a season of success?

Let me assure you, I thoroughly understand rejection. My life was a textbook example of brokenness. I have experienced the negative effects and baggage that accompany a rejected heart. In fact, for thirty years, rejection consumed my emotions, directed my thought patterns, and forced me into unnecessary crises. That was when my *aha* moment came, when I came face-to-face with the realization that rejection is unavoidable. Life presented me with two options: I could continue to fight the monster that was devouring my self-esteem, draining my passion for living, and undermining my ability to develop positive relationships. Or I could embrace rejection, work it to my advantage, learn how to extract my self-worth, and develop meaningful and lasting relationships. I chose the latter and have never looked at rejection the same way again.

I must warn you this book is not for those who enjoy wallowing in self-pity. The purpose is not to revisit the pain of rejection. The initial sting is painful enough. Rather, my purpose is to reveal the countless ways rejection can work for and not against you.

I am writing to those who have grown tired of others drawing the line of where their potential ends or weary of wearing labels others place upon their lives. I am writing to the broken person who remains paralyzed by fear that she will never measure up or has lived in the shadows of another's dream for so long she has forgotten her own. I am writing to someone who has experienced his fill of colorless dreams, dead-end opportunities, failures, frauds, and phonies. I am writing because I believe someone has encountered great heartache, pain, and suffering, yet against all odds has refused to let the dream within her heart die. If this in any way describes you, then this book is for you.

> My purpose is to reveal the countless ways rejection can work for and not against you.

The principles in this book have the potential to launch you into the greatest season of your life. They are foundational to identifying your purpose and will instruct you on how to maximize your potential. By reading this book, you will learn how to redirect your focus from what has been perceived as loss to discovering who and what qualifies as part of your future. You will learn how to make wise and decisive decisions. You will discover the value of mentors and will learn how to develop healthy relationships. You will understand the importance of developing a positive self-portrait by overcoming negative thoughts, fear, and lack of self-confidence.

> The principles in this book have the potential to launch you into the greatest season of your life.

Throughout this book you will read stories of men and women just like you who conquered the devastating blows of rejection. In every story, analogy, or lesson your spirit will be encouraged, and you will never view rejection the same way again. I will share with you wisdom I used to conquer the crushing blows of rejection, but only you can carry out the principles contained in this book. You must read, learn, and initiate action. The first step in winning the battle over rejection was purchasing this book. That first step shows you are serious about conquering rejection. I am confident that you will experience victory and success.

Before we begin, I must tell you that my beliefs and core values are rooted deeply in my faith and the Word of God.

Without God's unfailing love, my life would be a colossal failure. The wisdom of His Word not only saved my soul but transformed my life. It is upon this premise that I offer you hope and courage. As we begin our journey together, I pray you will explore the wisdom of God with a fresh perspective. He alone can restore the broken and hurting places of your life.

1

Rejection: Life's Golden Opportunity

*No one can make you feel inferior
without your consent.*

—Eleanor Roosevelt

Has your heart ever crumbled into a million pieces? Have you experienced the devastation of a broken vow, the grief of betrayal, the painful words of a friend, or discouragement from pursuing a dream? You are not alone. Life is not always easy, and rejection is real.

Rejection is more than a feeling, more than negative words, more than a fleeting emotion. It is a doubled-edged sword that shapes the future of the wise and destroys the focus of the undiscerning. To the optimist, rejection acts as a personal conductor, carefully arranging who and what qualifies for his or her future. For the pessimist, rejection becomes the archrival who destroys his or her purpose, the nemesis who steals joy, and the assassin who kills his or her dreams. Rejection is unavoidable. Your response to rejection, however, will determine your level of self-esteem, your passion for living, and your potential for positive relationships; and it will ultimately decide which doors of opportunity will be open to you.

POSITIVE ATTRIBUTES OF REJECTION

You must learn how to approach, confront, and work rejection to your advantage.

Rejection is more powerful than we dare believe. Therefore, you must learn how to approach, confront, and work rejection to your advantage. Understanding the positive attributes of rejection is the first stepping-stone to securing a successful future. The second is giving rejection permission to work on your behalf. Before we begin, I will list the top ten essential truths you must know about rejection.

TOP TEN TRUTHS ABOUT REJECTION

1. Rejection is simply the reaction or opinion of another person.
2. Rejection is powerless without your cooperation.
3. Rejection is a friend who withholds no secrets, exposes all enemies, and closes every wrong door.

4. Rejection is confirmation that you possess an achievable dream.
5. Rejection reveals those incapable of distinguishing your personal worth.
6. Rejection is a guide leading you away from dead-end relationships while directing you toward healthy, positive relationships.
7. How you respond to rejection is a reflection of your self-worth.
8. Rejection exposes who or what does not belong in your future.
9. Rejection reveals who is intimidated by your potential.
10. Rejection is motivation to go in a new direction.

Let's bring these truths into perspective. Take a moment and remember when you encountered rejection. Perhaps it was in a relationship, career, marriage, or among your peers. Vividly relive the moment. What was your reaction? How did you feel? How did you respond? Did you hide in a bed of depression for days? Did you defend your heart, justify your actions, or spew anger and bitterness? Or perhaps you sought comfort in the arms of a forbidden lover.

What does unbridled rejection do? It exposes every ounce of vulnerability and weakness we have buried inside. It will drive an ordinarily sane, rational person to say and do the unthinkable. Consider, there are thousands of intelligent, capable people sitting in a ten-by-ten prison cell because they took some illegal action when someone betrayed their trust and opened the wrath of their insecurities.

Is there hope? Is there a strategy for conquering rejection? Yes—you embrace it. Embrace rejection? That's right, embrace it. Make rejection your greatest companion. Rejection is a friend who withholds no secrets, exposes all enemies, and closes every wrong door. Right now you are probably thinking, *Surely I misunderstood. Are you telling me rejection is a good thing?* Rejection is more than good; it is one of life's golden opportunities. Rejection reveals, alerts, exposes, defines, confirms, and is one of the greatest motivators in life.

Those who conquer rejection understand two important principles. First, rejection is not about experiencing loss but rather discovering who or what qualifies for your future. Second, understanding rejection is a golden opportunity to further understand God's love, human relationships, and the gift of encouragement within you. Many times the wisdom born out of our personal crises becomes healing for someone else's pain.

BLINDSIDED BY REJECTION

Can I let you in on a personal secret? Growing up, the identity of my biological father remained a mystery. Did this affect me? Yes, profoundly. There are few things that cultivate the self-esteem of a girl more than her relationship with her father. For years I deeply desired to meet my father. Often, I would create make-believe scenarios of our first meeting.

I imagined my father taking me in his arms, telling me how much he missed me, and then offering to spend the rest of his life making up for the years we had been apart. That day never came. Anticipation turned into anxiety, longing into loneliness, and expectation into rejection. Decades of rejection eroded my self-esteem and left me with a broken and distorted identity. It took many years to discover the powerful truth that identity is not tied to a person, a career, or even accomplishments. Our identities are revealed when we discover who God has created us to be and what earthly assignment He has chosen us to fulfill.

It is probably safe to say I'm not the only one who's been blindsided by rejection. Am I correct in my assumption that you, too, have experienced unmerited rejection? How did you react to it? Did you close your eyes, hold your breath, count backward from ten, and pray for a miracle? Did you display an unrestrained tirade of rage or throw yourself facedown in your pillow and cry for days? Or were you one of the uncommon who embraced a dark moment with grace? Don't feel bad if your response was ill-mannered, even uncivilized. Rejection can have this effect. The truth is, rejection has left an imprint on your past. There are many who encounter rejection's sting, but few are courageous enough to acknowledge the power it has inflicted over their minds and emotions. Countless become hostages to rejection. Sadly, few receive the wisdom necessary to turn the tables on rejection.

As we begin our journey, I promise I will not attempt to

rationalize why bad things happen to good people. I know, firsthand, that the answers to life's most difficult questions are never easy to understand. What I have discovered is you can redirect the heartache of broken commitment and betrayal by using it to design a healthy and productive life.

You can redirect the heartache of broken commitment and betrayal by using it to design a healthy and productive life.

You can live beyond the hurt, pain, and isolation of a rejected heart. In fact, God delights in using the difficult and sometimes unexplainable circumstances of life to our advantage.

Let me share with you my feeble attempts of trying to evade rejection. Having encountered severe rejection at an early age, I did everything possible to escape situations or avoid relationships that could end in rejection. I ran. I hid. Rejection sought me, found me, and won every time. Why? Because rejection preys upon the fearful. Fear is the fuel that drives insecurity, anxiety, and low self-esteem. You cannot hide from rejection; you must conquer it.

Since hiding was not the solution, I decided that surely I could outsmart rejection. During the next phase of my life, I asserted my rights as an adult, drew boundaries, narrowed my scope of relationships, and left others before they had a chance to abandon me. This strategy worked for about a month. Then I was alone, cynical, and feeling more rejected than before.

Finally, attempting the intellectual approach, I attended

every seminar and conference that came through town. I bought every new self-help book hitting the market and read, underlined, and memorized. I reasoned that smart, successful, intelligent people do not have to deal with rejection—or do they?

We need only to read the headlines to see success is not the cure for rejection—if anything, it is the bullet within the loaded gun. What drives a straight-A student with a full athletic scholarship to take his life because his girlfriend breaks off their relationship? What internal chaos pushes a beautiful actress with numerous Academy Awards, a multimillion-dollar home, and a gorgeous husband who idolizes her to be in and out of rehab? Few would believe she, of all people, fights nagging voices telling her she is last month's news or her best days are behind her and her looks are fading quicker than the Los Angeles sunset.

You cannot hide from rejection; you must conquer it.

From the crack house to the country club, rejection touches everyone. I know people who are constantly in and out of romantic relationships. What compels them to get into one relationship after another? The unpleasant voice of rejection is the instigator. Rejection whispers in her ear, *Without a man you are incomplete.* Desperate to have a man, any man, if it will divert her lonely feelings of being unloved, she falls for the first man who comes along. She dates but feels incompetent to meet his needs, so she leaves, looking for someone who will fill the void created by rejection. Like many others, she falls for the mirage that somewhere, in a relationship just beyond her grasp, lies the forbidden fruit of happiness.

CONFRONTING AND CONQUERING

If you cannot hide from it, maneuver around it, avoid it in relationships, or intellectualize beyond it, how then do you handle rejection? The key to conquering rejection is learning how to turn it into the greatest motivator in your life. There are two types of people: the conquered and the conquerors. The conquerors confront rejection and make it their ally. The conquered hide in fear and refuse to contest the validity of rejection's lies. The simple truth is, rejection will either conquer you or you will conquer it.

> The key to conquering rejection is learning how to turn it into the greatest motivator in your life.

A clearly defined self-identity is the first step toward embracing rejection as a golden opportunity. In the next chapter we will study the intricate struggles of a rejected heart, but first we need to examine the root of every heart issue—the fight for identity. The identity crisis sweeping our country is astounding. The other day I watched the documentary of a well-known actor's daughter as she declared herself transgender. During an interview she claimed she was genetically conceived as female but is mentally and emotionally male. The focus of the

documentary was to persuade viewers to explore the possibility that your
birth gender could be a mistake. This
philosophy stands in direct opposition
of biblical truth. Refuse to buy into the
lie you are anything less than God's
perfect creation, fearfully and wonderfully fashioned by
the Creator of the universe. God did not make a mistake
when He created you.

God did
not make
a mistake
when He
created you.

Be an Original

I once had a friend who bought everything I bought. If I
purchased a pink suit, she purchased a pink suit. If I bought
black stilettos, she bought black stilettos. At first it was flat-
tering, then it became exasperating. Over time, it became
difficult for others to discern who was imitating whom.
Those suffering from negative feelings of rejection often find
it difficult to create a personal sense of style, mannerism,
speech, or even circle of friends. At some point, someone,
either through action or verbal expression, conveyed the
message, "Your opinion is worthless." In that moment, their
hearts received a message of disqualification, and the flow
of divine creativity began to diminish.

People who live in fear and lack authenticity will often
wilt at the first sign of opposition or disapproval. They
dread others won't accept their thoughts, ideas, or suggestions, and fear undermines their self-confidence. Gradually

the ability to express original ideas will be substituted for more conventional viewpoints others find acceptable.

Do you have a clear picture of who you are to become? Do you recognize your value? Have you discovered your personal worth? There is a wealth of potential within you, and it is time for you to discover it.

IDENTITY: WHO AM I REALLY?

I am amazed how a word of admiration or expression of affirmation can create energy that lasts for days. I don't know about you, but a compliment can change my entire day. Positive affirmation creates energy and confidence. Admit it, when a total stranger walks up to you and says, "Girl, I love your shoes. Where in the world did you find those?" you feel good. Inside, you're thinking, *Yes, they are adorable aren't they? I made a good choice. I have great taste. In fact, I should be a professional stylist.* One compliment can empower you to take on the world.

> Rejection is a serious issue, but with wise discernment, time, and effort, an optimistic heart can emerge.

Conversely, I have watched words of rejection destroy a person's self-esteem, potential, or dream forever. Rejection is a serious issue, but with wise discernment, time, and effort, an optimistic heart can emerge. Possessing a clear and definitive identity of who you are will leave little room for the envious, cynical, skeptical, or jealous opinions of others. Before you can conquer the negative words from others, you must first conquer your own negative thoughts. For the remainder of this chapter I want you to develop a renewed identity of who God has created you to become.

House of Mirrors

Children have a way of bringing life into perspective. When our children were young, they insisted on going to the local fair. One of their favorite attractions was the house of mirrors. Fascinated by the warped images the mirrors provided, they would run from mirror to mirror as each showed a new distortion of their true reflections. While one mirror made them look exaggeratedly tall, the next gave the appearance of being extremely wide. The more bizarre the shape, the more they laughed. The fun lasted until they gazed into the final mirror. There they looked up and questioned, "Is that what I really look like?" They had looked at so many distorted views of themselves that by the end of the maze they had forgotten their true appearance. What about you? Have you looked into the mirror of others' perceptions for so long you have forgotten your true image? A misconstrued image of one's self is the cause of poor self-esteem, fear, self-doubt, and negative thinking.

Your self-esteem is a mirror image of self-perception. If distorted, that mirror can create an unhealthy self-portrait and sabotage any undeveloped potential for success. What is your self-portrait? Is it positive? Is it an accurate description? If I were to spend an hour interviewing your closest friends, how would they depict you? What words or stories would they use to illustrate your personality? Those who have successfully defeated rejection embrace a healthy self-image, while the unsuccessful remain trapped by the warped image of who others wish them to become. How you view yourself will ultimately decide how you live your life.

Years ago, a famous singer and songwriter made a powerful point about self-worth. When asked during an interview, "What keeps you from competing to be number one?" she confidently replied, "Because I know no one can be a better *me*, than *me*." Sincerely humble, yet boldly confident, she understood that when you are simply yourself, the costly spirit of competition withers and self-confidence emerges.

Role-Playing

A person who fears rejection often develops a people-pleasing personality. Eager to gain or keep the approval of others, they fall into an approval-based performance trap. For some, the need for acceptance is so strong they adapt their personality to fit the role or image others find desirable. Becoming emotional actors or actresses, they take on roles of various personalities, professions, occupations, or even false identities, if it means gaining the approval of another. They willingly do whatever it takes to make others happy.

This identity crisis often continues until they grow weary of playing the part and subsequently begin to blame others for forcing them to become something they are not.

Not long ago, I took a mini vacation to Branson, Missouri. Branson is known as a small town with big shows. The shopping is excellent, and overall the shows are superb. The twenty-mile stretch of road leading into Branson is saturated with posters, signs, and various forms of advertisement announcing showtimes and headliners.

On this particular trip, I noticed a large billboard displaying the faces of famous musicians and recording artists. The top of the billboard read, "Today you can see the legends all in one convenient location." Upon arriving at the hotel, I was given complimentary tickets to the two o'clock show. The theater was small, the stage dimly lit, and the auditorium smelled musty. At ten minutes past two the drum roll began, the curtain went up, and out walked Elvis, or at least someone they wanted us to believe was Elvis. Like clockwork, every ten minutes, the audience was introduced to another impersonator of a true legend. This was perhaps the most unpleasant hour of entertainment I have ever experienced. Remember, no one appreciates a cheap copy of a great original.

Authentically You

At some point we all have been defined by the superficial labels others have ascribed to us. As a society, we encourage free speech and opinion. Opinions are power-ful. They are key factors creating the framework of our identities. However, this freedom, if used in a negative way, encroaches on our personal development. Consider a time when others branded you as ordinary, unintelligent, old, poor, or perhaps void of potential. How impactful were their words? Words become the framework of our futures. There will be many voices seeking to judge and define your significance. Remember, *who* defines you is as important as *how* they define you. Opinions do matter. What others think and say about you will influence how you feel.

I want you to discover the *real you*. Not who others have said you are, but the real you. Remove the mask for just a moment. Peel back the layers of expectation and the unend-ing demand for approval. Who are you beneath the pressure and pain? Have you forgotten?

Let's step back and rediscover the real you, the *original you*, without any heartache, before the negative opinion of others and minus the ill-effects of rejection. In the next few chapters I am going to share with you multiple ways you can reverse the negative effects of rejection, turning them into positive life principles. Get your pen and highlighter ready; these truths will reveal what the naysayers and killjoys do not want you to discover. If you are ready to climb out of the pit of rejection, then follow me to chapter 2 where we will uncover the truth about rejection.

Chapter Principles

1. Rejection acts as a personal conductor, carefully arranging who and what qualifies for your future.
2. Rejection is a friend who withholds no secrets, exposes all enemies, and closes every wrong door.
3. Rejection is a golden opportunity to better understand God's love, human relationships, and gifts of encouragement that lie within you.
4. Your reaction to rejection is a reflection of your self-worth.
5. Rejection is an opinion and only has power when received as truth.
6. Fear is the fuel that drives insecurity, anxiety, and low self-esteem.
7. Confront rejection and it will quickly become your ally. Left uncontested, rejection will devour you.
8. A clearly defined self-identity is the first step in embracing rejection as a golden opportunity.
9. Rejection reveals, alerts, exposes, defines, confirms, and is one of the greatest motivators in life.
10. When warped by rejection, your personal perception can create an unhealthy self-portrait and sabotage any undeveloped potential.

Words of Wisdom

I have loved you with an everlasting love; therefore
I have continued my faithfulness to you.

—Jeremiah 31:3

Power Quote

Believe in yourself and there will come a day when
others will have no choice but to believe with you.

—Cynthia Kersey

Plan of Action

Take a moment and consider your worth. Make a list of
all the remarkable attributes God has placed within you.
Be sure to focus on the qualities that make you unique,
including gifts and talents. Now place this list somewhere
easily accessible and read it often, memorizing it if possible.
Focusing on who God created you to become will guard
your heart in times of crisis or when you feel vulnerable to
negative thoughts or opinions.

2

Conquering the Need to Be Perfect

A positive attitude may not solve all
your problems, but it will annoy enough
people to make it worth the effort.

—Herm Albright

Dr. Seuss's book *How the Grinch Stole Christmas* is a fabulous illustration of how a heart, when damaged by rejection or betrayal, finds it difficult to receive love. Think of someone who reminds you of the Grinch. You know the one I am talking about, the person who seems aloof, standoffish, a loner, or an overall killjoy? I suspect the person you are thinking of possesses other personality traits that are Grinch-like in nature. For instance, they may act suspicious, guarded, or hypersensitive when it comes to forming new relationships, or spew forth negative, fault-finding words of criticism.

I am sure everyone knows a least one Grinch-like person who finds it difficult to understand unconditional love. In all likelihood that person struggles with the concept that others are capable of loving him "just because." Although his heart may be callous and cold, it doesn't mean he is incapable of changing. The one who broke through the icy exterior of the hideous, self-absorbed Grinch was a little girl named Cindy-Lou Who. With outstretched arms and caring questions she cracked open the door of the Grinch's hardened heart. I am thoroughly convinced every Grinch needs a Cindy-Lou, someone willing to peel back the crusty layers of cynicism and find the heartbeat of a hurting person.

Perhaps, like the Grinch, your heart has grown callous, hardened by the hurtful words of others or the sting of relationships gone wrong. I feel confident the percentage of people who have permitted their heart to grow dull from heartache is higher than one could imagine. I am also confident that overly protecting our hearts is one of the dangerous side effects that accompany a rejected heart. Below I have listed seven symptoms that identify a heart wounded by rejection. Please take time to read these symptoms aloud, asking, "Do I have the symptoms of a wounded heart?"

Symptoms of a Damaged Heart

1. A damaged heart rarely feels accepted.
2. A damaged heart attempts to protect itself from future pain.

3. A damaged heart struggles to attain perfection.

4. A damaged heart has trouble trusting others.

5. A damaged heart has difficulty receiving love.

6. A damaged heart feels inadequate.

7. A damaged heart demands loyalty.

How many of the above characteristics describe you? Do you fit the profile of having a wounded heart? If so, the first thing you must do is admit your heart has been wounded. I am not sure why, but the first step is often the hardest. It is often difficult to admit we are somehow flawed, wounded, or damaged. Be honest enough to confront rejection head-on. Admit to yourself, *Yes, I am wounded* and *No, I am not perfect.* Confession is very significant. It opens the door and allows the healing process to begin.

The bottom-line truth is, every wounded heart needs healing. I want to begin our healing journey by discussing the issue of unworthiness. Unworthiness means to dishonor or discredit one's abilities through actions or words. It is the opposite of self-confidence. Please note, I did not say arrogance; I said confidence. Is there a difference? Yes. Arrogance is an outward expression of false confidence. Meditate

> The bottom-line truth is, every wounded heart needs healing.

on that statement. If arrogance is a counterfeit, it must work overtime to compensate for lack of genuine confidence. In contrast, true confidence emerges from the inside and flows to the outside.

This point brings us back to the issue of unworthiness. A lack of self-confidence is a significant sign that a person suffers feelings of unworthiness. Remember you cannot exude genuine confidence on the outside while feeling unworthy on the inside. If you mistreat yourself through actions or words, others will feel comfortable doing the same. Self-depiction is powerful. How you speak to yourself and about yourself is an overall indication of your self-image. Your words are a canvas upon which you paint your self-portrait. Your verbal description will become the standard of how others think and feel about you, ultimately determining how they respond to you. One way to transform rejection into a powerhouse of potential is to change your self-depiction.

PURE LOVE

One Christmas, I received a Raggedy Ann doll. I loved her from the moment I opened the package. My Raggedy Ann received my time, attention, and all the unconditional love a five-year-old could offer. Yet she offered little in return: no food or shelter, no intellectual or emotional interaction, and she possessed no monetary value. Although thousands of little girls had Raggedy Ann dolls, I loved her because she was mine.

Why did I tell you this story? Because I want you to understand it is possible to experience unearned, unmerited love. Perhaps a series of relationships gone wrong have left you struggling to believe someone could love you and never leave you. Or could love you with no strings attached.

Before we move forward, take a moment to answer the following questions:

- Do I create a mental checklist of things I must do or say to qualify for love?
- Do I look for reasons not to be loved or accepted?
- Do I feel unworthy when others publicly congratulate my work or honor my accomplishments?
- Do I feel embarrassed or overwhelmed when someone throws me a surprise party?
- Do I feel guilty when given an expensive gift?

If you answered yes to more than two of the above questions, then pay close attention to the principles outlined in the next few paragraphs.

WHY DOES GOD LOVE ME?

"Why does God love me?" is a question I hear often from those who have experienced tremendous rejection. People who have encountered rejection can find it difficult to understand or embrace the love of God. Those who feel guilt over something they have done feel unqualified to receive His love.

God's love is not based on our good works but on His grace.

God's love is not based on our good works but on His grace. By reading 2 Corinthians 9:8 we better understand God's love—specifically, how it comes to us in the beautifully wrapped package of grace. "And God is able to provide you with every blessing in abundance, so that by always having enough of everything, you may share abundantly in every good work." If God's love depended on our perfection, no one would qualify for His love.

Those who have experienced the painful sting of rejection often have difficulty distinguishing their works from God's grace. Our works, regardless of how magnificent they may seem, are incapable of earning God's love. The truth is, "God is love" and He yearns for us to receive His undeserved love (1 John 4:8).

POSTER GIRL

I have a friend who is young and outgoing. Let's assume her name is Kris. Kris could be the poster girl for any high-end fashion boutique. She is sassy, slim, and smart. On the surface she appears confident and self-assured, but over the years I have noticed one distinct flaw: she is masterful at giving compliments but is incapable of receiving one. If you were to compliment Kris on her shoes, she would respond, "Thank you—but don't you think they make my feet look big?" If you were to say, "Wow, what a great picture of you," she would say, "I don't think so; I'm not very photogenic." Kris always finds a way to challenge or negate any compliment.

One day I asked Kris, "Why can't you simply receive a compliment?" At first she denied the fact and swiftly changed the subject. But a few weeks later, she cautiously addressed the issue. She opened up about her relationship with her mother, explaining that as a child she found it difficult, if not impossible, to please her. Kris went on to say every time someone gave her a compliment, her mother would counter the compliment with a negative comment. For instance if a neighbor complimented her on being a nice young lady, her mother would add, "Well, I guess she is good, at least some of the time." Until my confrontation with Kris, it never occurred to her she had taken on the negative trait of her mother, subconsciously undoing any words of affirmation or encouragement.

The number one reason we are highly critical of ourselves is because someone in our past has trained us to indulge in self-hatred.[1] The question is, why are we still listening to the voice of negativity? If you have nurtured inaccurate voices from your past, stop. Begin to renew your mind with positive, life-giving words. A surefire way to reverse any negative effects of rejection is to retrain your mind to think and then speak words of affirmation. If you are going to transform rejection into a positive, you must think positive thoughts and speak encouraging words. Remember, your

> If you have nurtured inaccurate voices from your past, stop. Begin to renew your mind with positive, life-giving words.

words, not the destructive words of others, will create your self-portrait.

THINGS COMPLIMENTS CAN'T FIX

As a child, I could not shake the feeling that somehow I wasn't good enough. Although I always tried my best, I felt as if I should have done more. My mind was a battlefield as I tried to measure up to the *perceived* expectations of others. I purposefully stress the word *perceive* because our perception is often distorted and unrealistic. Those who struggle with perfectionist tendencies are acutely aware the most critical voice in your life is the one within your mind. Please trust me when I tell you, the judgmental and fault-finding voice sputtering away in your mind will not go away without a fight. After dominating your feelings far too long, negative thoughts will not relinquish the reins and simply walk away. Because your internal voice reveals self-perception, it will take time to replace negative thoughts of rejection with positive thoughts of acceptance. Can this mountain be conquered? With absolute certainty, I proclaim, yes!

> It will take time to replace negative thoughts of rejection with positive thoughts of acceptance.

If you are going to replace the outdated self-portrait painted with broken brushes and colorless dreams, you must transform your actions and reactions. How you talk to yourself shapes how you feel about yourself. For example, when you do something clumsy, awkward, or forgetful, how do you respond? When you walk into a meeting with toilet paper streaming from your stilettoes, or spend twenty minutes looking for your sunglasses only to discover they are on top of your head, what names do you call yourself? What is your first response? Is it positive? If not, I want you to sit down and make a list of positive ways to describe yourself. Be specific. Take time to discover what you like about yourself. Remember, others will never find you desirable until you do. Self-confidence is magnetic.

ALL SELF-TALK IS SIGNIFICANT

A million compliments cannot cure negative self-talk. That is the reason self-talk is perhaps the most influential conversation in your day. Psychology proves we maintain incessant and unbroken conversations with ourselves daily. Although these internal conversations are usually silent, they are powerful.[2] The reason self-talk is so powerful is because there is not an outside voice of reason. There is no one to govern our words or weigh them for accuracy. Lies and distortions of truth can go unchallenged because there is no one to question their validity.

Internal dialogue accounts for most of all decision-making. What you think and how you feel usually determine what you do next. You spend more time with yourself than with anyone else. You are your constant companion and will spend a lifetime conversing with yourself. Your greatest influence will be—that's right—you. Your internal dialogue will be the most significant voice in your life. It will determine your attitude, goals, and overall happiness.

Turn Wrong Thinking Inside Out

For decades, I was my greatest critic. I had a hidden filing system of negative slurs, fault-finding phrases, and self-indulgent insults. Whatever the situation, I had a surefire system of reasons I could not measure up or was guaranteed to fail. I believed my own lies and slander. I thoroughly convinced myself I was ugly, dumb, incompetent, and hopeless. The question haunted me, *Why did I do this? Why did I feel the need to undermine my worth?* The more important question was, would I ever be able to stop the flow of negative self-talk?

The ugly truth was, I had not been thinking or expressing the thoughts of God. Although gifted to encourage and motivate others, I struggled to speak positive words over my life. I felt helpless, uncertain if I would ever be able to change my negative self-perception. Sure, I was great at re-creating the self-image of others, and I was known for empowering others with my words; yet I still had not learned how to talk to myself. All the years of training, self-help books, and seminars, and I still struggled to feel loved and accepted. I could blame others for my condition, but deep inside I knew the blame game wouldn't work and my only hope would be trusting God to turn my wrong thinking inside out.

What about you? Have you been your worst critic? Do you find yourself speaking negative, fault-finding words to yourself? If so, I encourage you to begin retraining your mind to think positive thoughts, to speak God's Word, and to embrace His will for your life. At first it may seem difficult, if not impossible, to undo years of wrong thinking. But with prayer and patience, you can develop a new mind-set and attitude. Take time each day to dwell on the positive principles contained in God's Word, retrain your mind, and guard your tongue, and soon your attitude and outlook on life will be more positive as well.

I encourage you to begin retraining your mind to think positive thoughts, to speak God's Word, and to embrace His will for your life.

Renew Your Mind

How do you renew your mind?

First, replace negative thoughts with positive ones. Positive thoughts create a heightened level of optimism and self-confidence. Negative thoughts produce destructive feelings or emotions which eventually form negative attitudes.

Second, make a list of positive self-descriptive words. Remember to substitute those words when tempted to use negative words instead. For instance, when you do make a silly or ridiculous statement, substitute the word *comedian* for *fool*. When you do things differently than others, quit labeling yourself a *misfit*; instead consider yourself *eccentric* or *nonconformist*. If you are a person who thinks out of the box, don't refer to yourself as an *oddball* but rather a *progressive thinker*. It may sound impractical, but it works.

Third, focus on the things you do well. List all the things that make you unique, and boldly embrace those characteristics. Gradually, you will retrain your mind to think in a healthy, balanced way. Philippians 4:8 provides us with the following guidelines:

> Finally, beloved, whatever is true, whatever is honorable, whatever is just, whatever is pure, whatever is pleasing, whatever is commendable, if there is any excellence and if there is anything worthy of praise, think about these things.

THE NEED TO BE PERFECT

Are you a perfectionist? A perfectionist believes everything should be done perfectly, without error or discrepancy. Recently, I watched an episode of a popular sitcom where the main character, the boss, employed a polite, good-natured young man to do small jobs around the office. Throughout the day, the boss would stop by and inspect the progress of his employee's projects. Oddly, the young man would be doing a wonderful job but would unexplainably make a mess or inadvertently ruin the project as soon as the boss appeared. The boss eventually learned his employee was suffering from performance anxiety. As long as no one watched him work, he performed well. However, the fear of someone scrutinizing or rejecting his work immobilized his creativity and kept him from completing his tasks. As I watched this episode, the truth became all too clear: perfection is elusive.

Try as hard as we might, we will never come close to hitting the mark of perfection. To help identify if you are striving for perfection, I have compiled a simple quiz. Please take a moment to answer the following yes-or-no questions.

ARE YOU A PERFECTIONIST?

1. Do you constantly focus on your personal imperfections, deficiencies, shortcomings, or failures?
2. Do you refuse to start a task that cannot be finished quickly and without interruption?
3. Are your personal expectations exceedingly higher than others'?
4. Do others perceive you as prideful, possessing a "better than thou" attitude?
5. Do you refuse to announce goals or projects for fear you will fail?
6. Are you reluctant to change set patterns or daily routines?

If you answered yes to three or more of the above questions, then you are definitely a perfectionist. One of the

identifying traits of a perfectionist is the prevailing attitude that says, "If I can't do it right the first time, I won't
do it at all." Consider the fierce competitor who refuses to
take part in an activity unless he is guaranteed to win. How
about the leader who feels overly responsible for failure
and carries any excessive sense of guilt that he should have
done more? Or the woman who turns down job promo-
tions because she is afraid of failing at the next level? She
feels her work is flawed, never good enough; and sadly, her
potential remains hidden beneath the rubble of insecurity.

Is there hope for the perfectionist? If so, what are the
steps to living a more balanced life?

Steps to Overcoming Perfectionism

I admit it: I am a perfectionist. My motto is, "I want things
done right, and I want them done yesterday." While there
is nothing wrong with maintaining high expectations, it is
important to develop balanced attitudes by creating realis-
tic and achievable goals. Here are a few examples of how to
balance out the perfectionist personality and avoid chronic
burnout.

Develop Achievable Goals

Challenging a perfectionist to set achievable and
reasonable goals is like asking a child to take only one bite
of his ice cream cone: difficult but not entirely impossible.
The dilemma most perfectionists face is the proclivity

to overdo, overthink, and overachieve, which unleashes a Pandora's box full of negative emotions, rejection, and eventually depression. When faced with a challenge, resist the urge to attempt too many tasks or to place unrealistic demands on your time or emotions. Learning to manage your schedule by setting reasonable goals guarantees a higher rate of success and a more balanced you. Discern your limitations. Allow room for flexibility, occasional mistakes, and moments to simply enjoy the journey.

Relax

If you are like most perfectionists, you experience an extraordinary need for structure and order. While this makes for a tidy house, it also generates high levels of stress that make you feel agitated, rigid, and uptight. Others will find you more enjoyable when you do not take yourself too seriously. Learn to laugh at unavoidable mistakes. Loosen the mental control of having to be perfect. Above all, remember to schedule at least a half hour of unplanned time each day to simply relax and unwind. Schedule time away and take a vacation when necessary. Be assured your family, friends, and colleagues will enjoy the refreshed and energized you.

Embrace Change

Let's face facts. Perfectionists are generally inflexible to change. As a matter of fact, the drive to have everything in perfect order resists change. Change, however, can be good, as it generates both creativity and imagination. There is a healthy balance between obsessive-compulsive and outright lazy. Balance begins by understanding every segment of your life does not need to be micromanaged. Life is not an exhausting sprint to the finish line. It will not fall apart if you miss a deadline, forget to take the trash out, or leave a spoon unwashed. Challenge yourself to take part in noncompetitive activities and enjoy them. Begin by learning to enjoy you. Forgive your past mistakes, admit you are human, and look forward to a new and exciting day.

Chapter Principles

1. True confidence cannot be counterfeited. You may exude confidence on the outside while feeling unworthy on the inside.
2. Words are a canvas upon which you paint your self-portrait.
3. Your verbal self-description becomes the standard of how others think about, feel toward, and respond to you.
4. If you mistreat yourself through actions or words, others will feel comfortable doing the same.
5. The number one reason we are highly critical of ourselves is someone in our past has trained us to indulge in self-hatred.

6. Your words, not the destructive words of others, create your self-portrait.

7. The most critical voice in the life of perfectionists is their own.

8. A million compliments cannot cure negative self-talk.

9. Self-talk is the most influential conversation in your day.

10. Words create feelings, which generate emotions.

Words of Wisdom

The LORD is near to the brokenhearted, and saves the crushed in spirit.

—PSALM 34:18

Power Quote

Nothing splendid has ever been achieved except by those who dared believe that something inside of them was superior to circumstance.

—BRUCE BARTON

Plan of Action

Seize the next twenty-four hours to check your self-talk. When setbacks or failures occur, document your verbal response and the responses of others. Be sure to assess which seem more factual, honest, and sincere. Consider the correlation of mood swings and conversation. Remember, words create feelings, which generate emotions.

Now that you are more aware of how words shape your image, commit to talking to yourself in a more positive and constructive way. Begin congratulating yourself on making right decisions, carefully replacing destructive, critical talk with biblical, Christ-like conversation. Meditate on Philippians 4:13, which proclaims, "I can do all things through him who strengthens me."

3

If You Love Me,
Don't Leave Me

What lies behind us and what lies before us are
tiny matters compared to what lies within us.

—Ralph Waldo Emerson

Alicia remembers standing on the wooden porch steps
the day her mother told her she was going to visit a sick
neighbor. The truth was, there wasn't a sick neighbor, only
a boyfriend with an expensive car and the promise of a new
life. That was the last time Alicia saw her mother.

Joshua's father, a legendary football coach, was home
almost every night. The only problem was that he was physically present but emotionally unavailable. He was either on
the phone pursuing the next superstar recruit or strategiz-
ing for Saturday's game. Joshua had a coach for a father, but
never a father for a coach. He grew up feeling powerless to
win the competition for his father's attention and affection.

Whether in a physical or emotional encounter, everyone will cross paths with abandonment. For many, abandon-

Healing from abandonment begins by focusing not on what has happened but on how we respond when negative things do happen.

ment proves a negative, life-altering experience; others remain unscathed, and a rare few emerge strengthened by their bout with rejection. Why does being abandoned produce bitterness in the heart of one, yet leave another unaffected? The answer is not found in questioning *why* others leave. The answer is hidden in how one reacts when people choose to leave. Healing from abandonment begins by focusing not on *what* has happened but on *how* we respond when negative things do happen.

IDENTIFYING THE FEAR OF ABANDONMENT

Thinking about living without someone you love can be overwhelming. But for a moment, consider that very fact: what if your feelings become a reality? What if your children and grandchildren move across the country? What if your best friend dumps you for new friends? What if your spouse of twenty-five years decides to leave you for a girl half his age? Losing someone you love through rejection or death is difficult. Feelings of grief or betrayal can produce intense, even erratic emotional responses.

What then is the appropriate response to actual or

perceived fear? How do you handle harassing thoughts trying to convince you, *One day, those you love most will abandon you*? Or defeat the nagging feeling lurking in the pit of your stomach when you think about your children being lost or taken? How do you combat fearful thoughts of things that *have not* happened? What about the insecurity that sneaks into your heart when you see your wife talking to another man? Will your faith ever prevail over your fears? Can you conquer the fear of abandonment? As a matter of fact, yes. You can fight your fears and win. It will take time and effort, but you can overthrow the fears that seek to sabotage your joy. How do you begin? By taking the first step and unmasking the source of fear.

I knew a young woman who lived in constant turmoil and crisis. Over coffee one day I asked her to share her story. I noticed she continually used phrases like, "I am not good enough"; "No one ever stays in my life for long"; "I will never be happily married." The sad truth is she attracted what she confessed. She devalued her worth and created a self-fulfilling prophecy of destruction. What about you? Have you created an environment for your insecurities to thrive? If so, it is time to dethrone harassing thoughts that devalue your self-worth, ruin your relationships, and destroy your dreams. What you think about most determines your feelings and fears. Let's face it. Many people wrestle with abandonment issues, but few are willing to acknowledge the feelings of inadequacy and failure they experience as a result of being abandoned.

How and when does the fear of abandonment begin? To

answer this question, we must first consider the source of fear. There are two basic types of fear. The first is healthy fear. Can fear be healthy? Extremely healthy, as it stems from the reasoning part of the brain and warns of real or impending danger.[1] For example, healthy fear acts as a warning signal cautioning a child to look both ways before crossing the street. Or it rationalizes with a teenager not to accept his friend's dare to dive off a seventy-foot cliff. There are numerous benefits to healthy fear. On the flip side of the equation, unhealthy fear works against our better judgment. Stemming not from logic but from emotion, unhealthy fear plays tricks on one's ability to think sensible and balanced thoughts.

The easiest way to process feelings of fear is to consider their source. If you want to qualify your fears, ask yourself the following questions. *Can my fears be substantiated by facts? Are my fears replacing my faith? Am I fearful of things or situations that do not exist?* Remember, feelings born out of negative thinking create unnecessary anxiety. Negative thoughts produce negative feelings, and negative feelings are the source of unhealthy fear. Let me share an example.

A precious lady named Sue admits, "I have nightmares about my daughter falling into an abandoned well and being severely wounded, and I am unable to come to her rescue. The bizarre thing is I have never fallen into a hole, neither do I know anyone who has. Why I am overtaken by the fear I will be unable to help my daughter in a time of crisis?"

The struggle to identify feelings associated with the

fear of abandonment is difficult if not outright frustrating. Abandonment is a complicated issue. I have witnessed the devastation of relationships gone wrong and the injustice of victims who felt as if they deserved the heartache of abandonment. Although no one reacts to loss in exactly the same way, there remains one thread of commonality: few understand the impact abandonment has had upon their lives, especially when it comes to relationships.

Few people know how to deal with the emotional baggage that accompanies abandonment. That is why I have written this book, to share with you truths that will set you free from unnecessary fear, anxiety, and wrong thinking. It *is* possible to overcome the fears associated with abandonment. In fact, you can begin the journey to freedom right now. Learning how to recognize the symptoms and characteristics associated with the fear of abandonment will get you on the fast track to recovery. Are you ready to begin the journey? Then let's get started.

Clinging to the Familiar

One of the most apparent symptoms of someone suffering from the fear of abandonment is the overwhelming need to cling to what is familiar. In a desperate struggle to hold on to people or positions, they often drive away the very thing they wish to keep.

An all-star athlete, popular, and the class clown, Troy was the picture of health and happiness until the day he received the news his father had been killed in Iraq. No longer outgoing, he spends most of his days staring out the window, battling anxiety and fighting the fear of being left alone. Possessive of his friends and controlling his girlfriend's every move, Troy is a classic example of someone who is trying to use control as a way of preventing loss.

Troy is not alone. Those of us who have experienced the trauma of losing a loved one understand the impulsive urge to hold on tightly to those we love. While it is natural to fight for the people who mean the most in our lives, the need to feel secure in relationships is often taken to extremes. Consider my friend Beth, who carefully arranges parties, outings, and events so her friends, romantic interests, coworkers, and family never intermingle. Beth always goes to her office Christmas party alone. Her boyfriends never meet her family, and friends from the gym never meet friends from work. Life for Beth has become a three-ring circus, and she is the ringmaster. Why all the drama? She fears abandonment. Subconsciously she reasons, *If friends become disinterested or family proves unloyal, I have the assurance I will never lose everyone I love at the same time.*

You are probably thinking my friend Beth sounds complicated. She is. We all are. Anyone who has encountered the turbulent waters of rejection and fought to navigate his or her way to safety understands the fight for emotional survival. Is there hope? Are we capable of having normal, stable, healthy relationships? The answer is yes. But before I share with you ways to overcome the fear of abandonment, allow me to give you a few more illustrations of relationship fears.

Panic and Paranoia

On her way to work, Kim calls her boyfriend at 7:00 in the morning. She calls again at 7:30, this time leaving a voice message. By 8:45, with no sign of a returned call, slight annoyance turns into anger. She sends a text; no response. She proceeds to text fifteen times within thirty minutes, each message more threatening than the last. Kim immediately jumps to the conclusion her boyfriend is cheating with the new office worker down the hall. Through a blur of angry tears she drives across town and bursts into his office demanding an explanation, only to discover he had inadvertently left his phone at home.

Panic is a sign of fear and insecurity. The fear of being forsaken or discarded can trigger an otherwise rational person to jump to irrational conclusions. For instance, when Kim's boyfriend did not immediately reply to her calls or text messages, she feared he was cheating or no longer had romantic feelings for her. In truth, he had simply forgotten his phone.

How does a person break the vicious cycle of fear-based paranoia? How do you keep your mind from racing toward the illogical? First, take a deep breath and calm down. Throwing grease on the fire only fuels the flames. Remember to keep your composure. Take a moment and consider possible scenarios that portray a more positive outcome. Above all, remember love does not concentrate on controlling others but on controlling oneself. The Amplified Bible describes the attributes of love this way:

> Love endures long and is patient and kind; love never is envious nor boils over with jealousy, is not boastful or vainglorious, does not display itself haughtily. It is not conceited (arrogant and inflated with pride); it is not rude (unmannerly) and does not act unbecomingly. Love (God's love in us) does not insist on its own rights or its own way, for it is not self-seeking; it is not touchy or fretful or resentful; it takes no account of the evil done to it [it pays no attention to a suffered wrong]. (1 Corinthians 13:4–5)

Avalanche of Fear

Janice frantically paces the driveway. Five minutes before her daughter's curfew and no sign of headlights. *Where is she? What has happened?* Listening for emergency sirens, she searches for the phone. Fuming, she yells at her husband, "Why does she put me through this? She knows how much I worry about her safety. If she misses curfew by one minute, she will not use the car for six weeks. I will not let her put me through this again."

The fact is Janice's daughter had never arrived home

late. Her mother, however, lived in full-throttle panic mode. Fear and anxiety were Janice's best friends. She was a drama queen on steroids. Expecting the worst in every situation, she was a whirlwind of stress and apprehension. When her children were young, she was terrified they would be lost, taken, or tragically wounded. Sadly, the only thing Janice's worrying accomplished was making her family miserable. Although she later admitted many of her fears were unreasonable, she still struggles to control her feelings of being separated from her daughter. The fear of losing someone due to an accident, disease, or death is more common than you might think.

A mother admits, "My irrational fear is that one of my children will bleed to death. Whenever they hold scissors or a sharp object, I'm concerned they will sever an artery and I will be unable to get them to the hospital in time."

A grandfather confesses, "I have a fear my grandchildren will get trapped in a car or an old freezer and will suffocate."

Years ago the term *worrywart* described a person who was negative, critical, and overly anxious. I had a relative who fit this description; to label her a pessimist would be a gross understatement. She had the flair for making a wedding feel like a funeral, and holidays with her were as joyous as eating glass.

Addicted to chaos, worriers focus on what could go wrong. The other day I had an interesting conversation with a lady who spent hours voicing one fearful thought after another. A few minutes into the conversation, I felt as if someone had shaken a two-liter soda bottle and released the cap. She talked about the economic recession and how she feared losing her job. The next topic was cancer, then the fear her husband would cheat, then her anxiety that her grandchildren would be harmed at daycare. Her life was an avalanche of fear, and she sat by waiting for it to fall.

Jumping and Dumping

Attractive, charming, and an emotional game player, Michael is notorious for jumping from relationship to relationship. He talks a good game in front of his friends and brags about his sexual exploits. On the surface he appears together and in control, but behind the shallow exterior of his bravado lie hidden insecurities. The truth is Michael is afraid of being dumped. Unable to form emotional bonds of commitment, he chooses to jump out of relationships to avoid being rejected.

Most toxic relationship patterns stem from the fear of being abandoned. In fact, it is common for a person who fears rejection to subconsciously attract those who are likely to abandon them. Consider Joleen, who said, "I was in my late thirties and engaged to my fourth husband before I realized I suffered extreme abandonment issues. After cycling through an endless maze of dead-end affairs I finally came face-to-face with the truth. Addicted to destructive relationships, I was like a massive magnet, attracting wrong men and repelling good men. My fear of being left or losing someone I loved was the fuse igniting a powder keg of explosive relationships."

A-Minus Failure

Jessica looks at her paper then stares miserably at her feet. It was an A-minus. Questioning how in the world she missed two questions, she shuffles back to her seat, devastated her perfect A-plus record is ruined. High self-expectations can be constructive, but an overly competitive nature is often a telltale sign of internal anguish. The need to perform well is typically ingrained in our minds during childhood. For instance, an authority figure, perhaps a parent or teacher, may give extraordinary attention or rewards to those achieving high academic honors. Thus children equate accomplishment with acceptance, and a pattern of approval-based performance begins. Let me be clear. I am in total support of rewarding excellence. When our children perform a task well, we reward them accordingly. What I want to draw your attention to is the connection between anxiety and the fear of failure.

People who long for acceptance feel constant pressure to do or become more. They become convinced that if they collect enough friends, accrue enough wealth, or climb high enough on the corporate ladder, they become irreplaceable. Are you beginning to see the correlation between anxiety and acceptance? Good. Now let's probe a little deeper and talk about insecurity.

Loving and Leaving

Married to Zac less than six months, Heather discovered traces of lipstick on his shirt and a woman's phone number in his wallet. *All men cheat; none can be trusted*, she reasoned. The truth is, all men don't cheat. Unfortunately, Heather encountered one who did. Stereotyping people based upon a single experience will not improve the bad behavior of others. But living with doubt, suspicion, and cynicism will condemn you to a life of unhappiness. All people are not the same, and to stereotype them as such is flat-out unfair. Relationships are not always doomed to end poorly. Many thrive and, yes, there are those who live happily ever after.

Staring at the floor and biting her nails, Samantha timidly confessed, "I am afraid." "Afraid of what?" I asked. She said, "I am afraid my boyfriend will leave." "Why do you feel he will leave?" "I don't know. My daddy left when I was seven and no one explained why. I just feel like my boyfriend will do the same thing." Seventeen-year-old Samantha remained emotionally paralyzed by her fears as a seven-year-old. Her first romantic relationship was ruined by fear that all men she loved would eventually leave. Can you relate to Samantha's struggle? Have you been guilty of labeling people based upon a single personal experience? Would you feel comfortable with others treating you the same way? Give friends, colleagues, and potential romantic interests the opportunity to express their love and gain your trust. Do not let negative relationships of the past be the downfall of positive future relationships. Stop categorizing and start enjoying the benefits of healthy associations.

Lenny writes, "I worry about my wife cheating. We are both loving and committed to each other. There is no rational reason for me to feel suspicious or threatened. Our relationship has not changed, and neither of us has close friends of the opposite sex. We attend Bible study once a week, and I should feel totally secure in our relationship. Why am I worried and how do I quit obsessing about something that isn't happening?"

Perhaps, like Lenny, you realize your fears remain unfounded, yet you struggle to control feelings of fear and anxiety. Afraid to face your fears, you remained trapped, consumed by situations that rob you of peace and joy. The good news is, you can overcome your feelings in spite of how out of control they may seem. Fears may not vanish overnight, but with patience and persistence they will lessen over time. Confronting the fear of abandonment is perhaps easier than you have imagined. Below I have listed important keys that will help you overcome your fear.

> Do not let negative relationships of the past be the downfall of positive future relationships.

Keys to Overcoming Fear

- Share your fears of abandonment with someone you trust. Voice your fears to a friend, then ask that friend for positive yet honest feedback about the validity of these fears.

- Write down personal strengths that would enable you to thrive if faced with the challenge of living alone. Having a documented list of personal strengths reinforces confidence and self-assurance, especially when facing discouragement or disappointment.

- Stop dwelling on the past and move forward. Mistakes and wrong decisions are a part of life. Release the pain, move past negative memories, and begin again.

- Spend time with and enjoy those who recognize your worth. Quit obsessing about the one who left and focus on those who have stayed. Stop expending emotional energy in past relationships and begin investing in those who are a part of your future.

- Cast worry by the wayside. Worry is like cyanide: tasteless and highly toxic. Create an outlet for anxiety. Discover new interests and explore channels for personal creativity. Learn to paint, join a gym, or better yet, find someone in need and discover ways you can help better his or her life.

- Create a list of things you fear. Then beside the list of things you fear, create a list of correlating Scripture verses that will help you overcome any negative thoughts that create anxiety or fear. Let me help you get started.

  - "And those who know your name put their trust in you, for you, O Lord, have not forsaken those who seek you." (Psalm 9:10)

- "Be strong and bold; have no fear or dread of them, because it is the LORD your God who goes with you; he will not fail you or forsake you." (Deuteronomy 31:6)
- "For I am convinced that neither death, nor life, nor angels, nor rulers, nor things present, nor things to come, nor powers, nor height, nor depth, nor anything else in all creation, will be able to separate us from the love of God in Christ Jesus our Lord." (Romans 8:38–39)
- "If my father and my mother forsake me, the LORD will take me up." (Psalm 27:10)

Putting the above keys into practice will safeguard your heart and help you form healthy, satisfying relationships. If you've ever been in a relationship where you didn't feel comfortable expressing your feelings or ideas, take some time to think about what you really need and how you want to feel in your ideal relationship. It is important to know what makes you feel safe and secure. Being able to clarify your feelings will help you

> You are worthy of relationships where you feel loved, treasured, and appreciated.

recognize which relationships are worthy of pursing or preserving. You are worthy of relationships where you feel loved, treasured, and appreciated.

Chapter Principles

1. Healing begins by focusing not on *what* has happened but *how* we respond when negative things do happen.
2. The easiest way to process feelings of fear is to consider their source.
3. A key sign of someone suffering from the fear of abandonment is the overwhelming need to cling to what is familiar.
4. Those who fear abandonment often drive away the people or positions they wish to keep.
5. Panic is a sign of fear and insecurity.
6. The fear of being forsaken or discarded can trigger an otherwise rational person to jump to irrational conclusions.
7. Most toxic relationships stem from the fear of abandonment.
8. Stereotyping people based upon a single experience will not improve the bad behavior of others.
9. Living with doubt, suspicion, and cynicism will condemn you to a life of unhappiness.
10. Negative thoughts can become self-fulfilling prophecies of destruction.

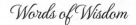

Words of Wisdom

I hereby command you: Be strong and courageous; do not be frightened or dismayed, for the Lord your God is with you wherever you go.

—Joshua 1:9

Power Quote

Fear cannot take what you do not give it.

—Christopher Coan

Plan of Action

There is comfort in knowing that when friends grow apart, children leave for college, or a spouse faces terminal illness, God will not leave or forsake us. When rooted in the promises of God's Word, we can face any crisis with the calm assurance of knowing God's love surrounds us daily. In an uncertain world where others may abandon us, God's love remains steadfast. Today, set aside time for the relationship that matters most, your relationship with God.

4

Divas, Deceivers, and Drama Queens

Negative people are worse than negative occurrences. The argument is over in ten minutes—the person may hang around for years.

—Jeffrey Gitomer

Diva . . . deceiver . . . drama queen—everyone has friends who fit these descriptions. Throughout life you will encounter fakes, phonies, attention grabbers, and liars, but some will be fortunate enough to discover a *diamond friend*. Rare, exquisite, and costly, a diamond friend can be hard to find. The good news is once they are discovered, these friendships usually last a lifetime.

After many friendships ended on a sour note, Maggie kept colleagues and acquaintances at bay. Fearful another relationship would end in rejection, she almost missed meeting Cynthia, who became a trusted mentor and life-long friend.

Although relationships seem complicated, the bottom-line truth is, many fit comfortably into either the category of being delightfully rewarding or extremely harmful. Because relationships play a big role in your personal success and overall happiness in life, it is extremely important to assess the value and validity of each relationship. My goal is to help you learn to use rejection as a guide leading you away from dead-end relationships while directing you toward healthy, positive relationships. As you read this chapter, be brutally honest in evaluating your most intimate relationships. Differentiate positive contributors from those who simply drain your creativity and disrupt your focus. In other words, separate the positive contributors from the leeches. Although a painful process, it will help you identify wrong relationships while highlighting productive ones. Before we journey forward, let's pause for just a moment to allow you to take a brief relationship inventory.

> Learn to use rejection as a guide leading you away from dead-end relationships while directing you toward healthy, positive relationships.

TAKE A RELATIONSHIP INVENTORY

The greatest of friendships are sometimes fragile. People are flighty—here today and gone tomorrow. Trying to meet the emotional needs of others is an overwhelming task, if not an outright burden. Routinely, I make a list of past, present, and potential relationships. I consider the pain of failed relationships while celebrating those that have proven positive and long lasting.

As you take the short quiz below, remember every relationship is an investment, yielding a rich reward or resulting in great loss. Therefore, make certain your answers are honest and accurate. Now, carefully consider the following questions:

- Who influences your day in a positive way?
- Who depletes your energy or resources?
- Whom can you entrust with your most intimate secrets?
- Who makes you happy? Challenges you? Nurtures you?
- Who is a worthy investment of your time?
- Who is genuinely excited when good things happen in your life?
- Who is jealous, intimidated, or envious when you succeed?

Let's be honest: we have made some rather hasty if not outright bad decisions when it comes to selecting friends or business associates. We have all had a friend who on the surface appeared excited and interested in every last detail of our lives, visions, or vocations. Is this friendship too good to be true? Honestly, nine out of ten times, yes! If you meet someone and immediately feel drawn into their world, it is a sure sign of one of two things: either God has a divine plan for your connection or the enemy does. Every relationship has a basis for its existence: either prosperity or destruction.

As we begin to wade our way through the murky waters of relationships, let's answer a few more questions. They will only take a moment, and the insights they offer will be worth the extra effort.

- What do you value most in a relationship? Is it love, trust, honesty, loyalty?
- How much emotional energy are you willing to invest in a relationship?
- Are your relationships usually short-lived or long-term?
- What boundaries do you set up in a relationship?

With these answers firmly in place, use rejection as a magnifying glass, illuminating the intentions of those around you. The answers provided will help you identify who qualifies for your future. Throughout this chapter we will amplify and discuss four types of relationships.

THE AFFIRMATION JUNKIE

Affirmation is addictive. Compliments are like an adrenaline rush: they offer a quick emotional high, but before long the effects begin to wear off, the downward surge begins, and the search for the next emotional fix begins. That is why compliments feel good: they create energy. Approval is the driving force in most relationships, especially in dysfunctional ones. It is both poison and pleasure to the brokenhearted. Let me give you an example.

I never will forget my high school friend Ginger. Ginger was cute, adventurous, funny, and highly successful—that is, in every area except relationships. Growing up, her parents were busy traveling the world and building careers, and sadly, Ginger's emotional needs were neglected. What I remember most about my friend was she was easily lured into wrong relationships by the verbal affirmation of those with impure motives. Throughout high school, she was drawn to every one-liner deceptive young men threw her way. Yearning for acceptance and addicted to approval, she was willing to do whatever it took to gain and keep the approval of others. Her need for attention was like a giant, overshadowing her good judgment and proving hard to defeat.

> Providing verbal affirmation to a rejected heart is like giving water to a person dying of thirst.

A powerful inoculation, affirmation immunizes the heart from unconstructive criticism. A healthy dose of encouragement will help safeguard the heart of those most susceptible to the negative effects associated with rejection. Providing verbal affirmation to a rejected heart is like giving water to a person dying of thirst. A wounded person craves positive words of encouragement. In fact, they can thrive on one rightly spoken word for months.

While affirmation in moderate doses can be benefi-
cial, an irrational need to please others can quickly lead to
unbalanced and unhealthy relationships. My friend Ginger
isn't the only one who has battled the giant of insecurity. I
have watched man after man abandon his wife and children
for a secretary who filled his ear full of flattery. I have heard
from teenagers who discarded their virtues for a night of
cheap, cookie-cutter compliments. The Bible is full of tragic
stories born out of emotional crises. Consider Cain, who
murdered his brother, Abel (Genesis 4:8). If we were to ask
Cain *why* he killed his brother, I am sure the answer would
be one word: *rejection*. The feeling that his offering was
unacceptable devastated Cain emotionally. In turn, Cain
took the life of someone he loved. Do you know someone
who reminds you of Cain? Someone who is destroying
his life or the life of someone he loves because he has not
learned how to respond to the voice of rejection?

One of the most challenging relationships in life will
be with the person who has experienced extreme rejection.
This is true because they subconsciously feel unworthy of
time, energy, or affection. Before long, those incapable of
receiving your love will deplete a large portion of your emotional energy.

Many years ago, I had an engaging friendship with a
female colleague. The first few months were pleasant, even
rewarding. However, before long I quickly realized maintaining our relationship would require more energy than I
had expected. At the onset of our friendship she expressed

the desire to assist me, working with various projects and freelance jobs when needed. What I did not detect was that she was very insecure. She required a continual stream of validation, affirmation, and conversation centered on her latest crisis. Instead of relieving my already strenuous workload, her insecurities added to it. Over the next few months, the person I had perceived as a mutual contributor in our relationship emerged as an emotional sponge slowly absorbing my energy. Before long I was forced to let her go, and our relationship ended on a sad note.

Is it possible to express your love and affirmation limitless times and in myriad ways only to have your sincerity questioned? Yes. Trying to affirm your commitment in an unhealthy relationship is like pouring water into a bag filled with holes. There will never be enough praise to fill a heart full of insecurity. The trouble is not your inability to express love but the bleeding heart that struggles to receive love. Sadly, without healing, those most ill-affected by rejection find it difficult, if not impossible, to stay in a healthy relationship. What is the remedy for insecurity? Do we simply abandon those who need us most? Do we sacrifice the ship and run for the lifeboats? Before we discover the solution, let's evaluate the problem more closely.

THE CONTROL FREAK

You love them but cannot handle them. Over-the-top, having to control everything, a little of a control freak goes a very long way. Do you have friends or family who fit this description? Do *you* fit this description? Okay, admit it, we all secretly want to be in the driver's seat of life. We can disguise the longing, masquerade it, or simply live in denial. However, the plain truth is that control makes us feel powerful.

From birth we quickly learn the art of manipulating and controlling our surroundings. Watch as a mother places her infant child down for an afternoon nap. Having fed, rocked, sang to, and gently caressed until the child is almost asleep, she places her in the crib, turns out the light, and tiptoes toward the door. As she pulls the door shut she hears a shrill, demanding cry that communicates, *No! Come back. I demand your time and undivided attention.* Frustrated and frazzled, the mother reaches down and cradles the infant in her arms. Immediately, the crying ceases. What transpired? A six-month-old just learned the skill and satisfaction of control.

Let's fast-forward thirty years. The infant, Rachel, a successful real estate broker in Florida, has a typical type A, overaccomplished personality. At work she is a fierce competitor. Among friends she becomes planner, organizer, and CEO of their social lives. As the acting director of vacations, events, and outings, she has assured every restaurant, cab ride, movie, and meal is prearranged. Known to monopolize the conversation and redirect when it does not appeal to her interest, Rachel plays the role of diva, drama queen, director, and chief of the fashion police.

What drives Rachel to control? After all, she is smart

and successful. She attracts men, but they leave as quickly as they come. Friends are initially lured by her enthusiasm for life, but few can survive her dominating nature. Relationships for Rachel are a revolving door of potential hopefuls, entering and exiting with rhythmic consistency.

Okay, it's time to confess. We either know a Rachel, or we are a Rachel. For those who have a friend or relative like her, remember that somewhere hidden beneath the tough exterior is a heart longing for acceptance. There is a wounded person whose trust has been broken or personal boundaries crossed. We all fight the fear of losing something or someone we love. In most cases we are simply trying to prevent more loss. Regardless of intentions, remember, no one enjoys being controlled.

For those who are courageous enough to admit they are control freaks, there is hope. Before we close this chapter, we will talk about ways to transform control issues associated with rejection. But first, let's discover how influential, if not entirely controlling, our family, friends, or coworkers have been about our decision-making. Go ahead and take the following quiz and evaluate if your relationships are healthy or simply disasters waiting to happen.

Am I in a Controlling Relationship?

1. Am I in a relationship where the other person makes all the decisions?
2. Do I often feel used for what I can do instead of being enjoyed for who I am?

3. Do I mentally retrace my conversations with others to ensure I did not say something this person would consider offensive?

4. Do I struggle to open up or speak my true feelings while in this person's company?

5. Are activities planned by this person, or do I share in the decision-making?

6. Does this person disregard my personal boundaries?

7. In the presence of friends or family do I feel nervous, anxious, or that I don't measure up intellectually or socially?

8. Do I find myself accommodating others' desires by participating in activities they enjoy rather than ones I enjoy?

9. Do I compromise personal responsibilities to make sure others are able to fulfill their project deadlines?

10. Does this person bring out my insecurities?

How did you do? If you answered yes to three or more of the above questions, then it is time you begin working toward emotional and relational freedom. You may ask, "Tracey, how do I handle an opinionated, boundary-breaking, self-assertive person?" First, recognize this person's need for acceptance. Controlling people are often hurting people who simply long to regain emotional balance in their lives. In their minds, the more things or people they can control, the less out-of-control their lives seem to be. Many times, an insatiable desire for control is an effort to restore balance in other areas in life. Divorce, death, bankruptcy, or loss in a relationship can create mental and emotional breaking points. Usually, those who exhibit control issues also struggle with chronic stress, obsessive-compulsive behavior, or rebellious tendencies. These are external behaviors reflecting underlying struggles of self-doubt, loss, and rejection.

Second, prayerfully remember their need for love. Nurturing, consistency, and reassurance will make a positive difference in their lives.

Third, set up and enforce personal boundaries. When family and close friends are involved, what defines healthy boundaries? How much space is considered appropriate? Where should privacy lines be drawn and to what extent should they be enforced? It is safe to say that, while the thoughts, opinions, and ideas of others should be an enjoyable addition to your world, they should not come with the high price tag of sacrificing your dreams. I assure you, I understand the manipulative tactics of those who will attempt to highjack your dreams. You would be surprised at the number of "take my word or else" pronouncements I have received over the years. Looking back, I now see the absurdity of such scheming threats. Granted, not everyone will agree with you all the time, but it is how they make you feel when they disagree that counts. Refuse to

> While the thoughts, opinions, and ideas of others should be an enjoyable addition to your world, they should not come with the high price tag of sacrificing your dreams.

engage in conversations where your thoughts are belittled or your feelings are dismissed. Remember, no matter how well-meaning others seem to be, emotional blackmail is always wrong.

Environment and associations shape your personal world. One of the major reasons people do not succeed in conquering the ongoing battle with rejection is they constantly expose themselves to the negative opinions of others. Find positive people and befriend them. Avoid negative, cynical, and jealous people at all costs. Surround yourself with creative, cheerful, encouraging people who have promising futures, and make them a part of yours. Learn to invest in who and what matters most. Wisdom and knowledge are all around you. Access them today by tuning out negative voices and replacing them with positive ones.

THE CRISIS RELATIONSHIP

There is a proverb that says, "The enemy of my enemy is my friend." How true. Nothing brings people together like a mutual enemy. Observe how two disgruntled employees, who have never liked each other before, receive termination papers on the same day. Suddenly, they rally together, joining forces to fight corporate headquarters. A common enemy, *pain*, became the matchmaker for an unforeseen relationship. Consider a time when you faced great tragedy. Who became your confidant? To whose arms did you turn for comfort? It is not uncommon for relationships to form from the ashes of painful experiences. I encourage you to evaluate the premise for every relationship. Keep in mind that the healthiest relationships are not formed out of past pain but out of future expectation.

> The healthiest relationships are not formed out of past pain but out of future expectation.

During a recent counseling session a woman tearfully complained, "I don't understand how people expect me to live with my alcoholic husband; he is loud, profane, and abusive." Then surprisingly, when asked about their courtship, she explained, "Well, I met my husband in a bar. We both enjoyed the club scene and for the most part, drinking was our only shared interest." Yes, this really did happen. Although it is tempting to shake our heads in disbelief, I suspect we have all missed the forest for the trees. As one who knows the heartache of dysfunctional relationships, I stress for you to remember that common strengths, not weaknesses, are the foundation for long-lasting relationships.

Another caution light of potentially damaging relationships is when a connection materializes at an abnormally fast pace, as if overnight. Ask a couple who have only known each other a few weeks why they are getting married so quickly. Very often, you will hear phrases like, "He gets me"; "She understands me"; "It's as if he can read my mind." Another commonly verbalized emotion is, "I feel like I have known this person my entire life." In many ways this is an accurate analogy. It is common for people who share similar backgrounds, experiences, or pain to share mutual attraction. Yet pain is often more attracted to pain than healing. Why? Because pain enjoys the companionship of dysfunction. Healing requires effort and energy. By exposing the darkened places of our insecurities, healing demands we change.

Why does a woman leave her faithful, loving husband for a two-timing, washed-up loser? Could it be her husband's wholeness challenges her insecurities? Or is it she feels more comfortable with a man who is equally dysfunctional? Maybe your spouse of twenty years has left you for a new fling, and you feel abandoned. The bitter sting of rejection is all too real. But I beg you to stop and consider for a moment, who should really bear the burden of abandonment? Should it be you, the one who feels betrayed, left behind? Or the one who broke trust and walked away? It is time to stop being emotionally imprisoned for crimes we have not committed. Break the chains, pick the lock, and walk free.

Lethal Conversation

The foundation of your future is your thought life. Thoughts are as vulnerable as they are valuable. For just a moment, consider the private conversation between Eve and the serpent in Genesis 3. It was perhaps the deadliest conversation in history. Now, before anyone judges Eve too harshly, keep in mind, conversations are keys that open doors to feelings. With that principle in mind, let's figure out how the enemy of God gained the trust of the daughter of God.

Every magician knows the first rule of deception: set the stage and prepare the mind to witness an optical illusion. With the skill set of a master illusionist, the serpent created an environment for the ultimate hoax, the grand delusion. Talking his way into Eve's future, he created a fanciful mirage and sold her a bill of goods. Replacing access with denial and blessings with curses, he pulled the slickest trick in the book, and the first woman fell for the infamous bait and switch.

Why did Eve fall into the web of deception? For the same reasons many fall for the smooth talker at work, the pick-up guy at the gym, or the lies of an unfaithful wife in their children's carpool. Eve believed the lie that God withheld from her information and approval. She bought into the notion that God shortchanged her opportunities and sabotaged her future. Talk about how deep the roots of rejection run! Let me be honest. I know, when it comes to rejection, this is perhaps the exception, rather than the rule. But sometimes rejection is more perceived than actual. Ouch, I know how the truth can sting. I am writing this because I have experienced the piercing prick of falsified rejection. That's right: *falsified rejection.* I know what you are thinking: surely the struggle with rejection is hard enough without throwing make-believe rejection in the mix. I wholeheartedly agree. I wish I did not have to address the issue either, but I must.

The secret to avoiding deception is learning to avoid sleight-of-hand conversation that makes perceived rejection seem real. A clear warning sign of dangerous conversation is when you leave feeling devalued or unappreciated. There is immeasurable difference in feeling inspired to reach for an unattained dream and the negative feeling a person is a stumbling block to your dream. Before we move on to the next point, let's analyze God's conversation with Eve more closely.

> Now the serpent was more crafty than any other wild animal that the LORD God had made. He said to the woman, "Did God say, 'You shall not eat from any tree in the garden'?" The woman said to the serpent, "We may eat of the fruit of the trees in the garden; but God said, 'You shall not eat of the fruit of the tree that is in the middle of the garden, nor shall you touch it, or you shall die.'" But the serpent said to the woman, "You will not die; for God knows that when you eat of it your eyes will be opened, and you will be like God, knowing good and evil." (Genesis 3:1–5)

In the above passage notice the electrifying speech the serpent gave Eve about her untapped potential. In essence he was saying, "I see what others have overlooked. I understand you. I want to make your dreams come true. I want to invest in you. Let me share wisdom others have withheld from you." Talk about a poser. He falsified Eve's future by painting a picture that dishonored her husband and made her question the motives of her Creator.

I challenge you to disengage from anyone who discredits godly authority or creates dissatisfaction in an otherwise healthy relationship. Now that you have learned how to identify wrong people in your present, it is time to assess who qualifies for your future.

THE IRREPLACEABLE RELATIONSHIP

E. W. Howe said it best: "When a friend is in trouble, don't annoy him by asking if there is anything you can do. Think up something appropriate and do it." If you really want to know who qualifies for your future, then remember a time when you experienced severe crisis. The one who stepped forward and turned a no into a yes definitely belongs in your future. A true ally highlights and extracts the best in you while gently correcting your faults. Faithful friends accentuate the positive and diminish the negative. They increase your strengths and diminish your weaknesses. They have witnessed your personality flaws firsthand yet choose to love you anyway.

- Discovering someone who cares about your dream is rare.
- Discovering someone who will invest in your dream is exceptional.
- Discovering a person who will sacrifice for your dream makes that person irreplaceable.

A true friend will never belittle your dream or diminish your energy toward fulfilling that dream. They ask only one question: "How can I help?" Think of a time you felt convinced you would not make it through a particular crisis. Who encouraged you most? Who offered wisdom and counsel? Did you choose to follow their advice? Why or why not?

Now write down the names of three trustworthy advisers. When is the last time you have consulted or accessed their wisdom? God places people in our lives today to reveal wisdom we need for tomorrow. Make sure you take full advantage of those who have the unique gift of mentorship. Consult, receive, and reward their wisdom accordingly.

> God places people in our lives today to reveal wisdom we need for tomorrow.

Chapter Principles

1. A wounded heart passionately pursues verbal affirmation and can thrive for months on one rightly spoken word.
2. Every relationship has a basis for its existence: either prosperity or destruction.
3. Affirmation is addictive. Compliments are like an adrenaline rush: they offer a quick emotional high, but before long the effects begin to wear off, the downward surge begins, and the search for the next emotional fix begins.
4. Approval is the driving force in most relationships, especially in dysfunctional ones. It is both poison and pleasure to the brokenhearted.

5. Trying to affirm your commitment in an unhealthy relationship is like pouring water into a bag filled with holes. There will never be enough praise to fill a heart full of insecurity.

6. A true ally highlights and extracts the best in you while gently correcting your faults. Allies accentuate the positive and diminish the negative.

7. Evaluate relationships, asking, "Is this person a contributor to my dream?"

8. The healthiest relationships are those that support a mutual flow of contribution and commitment.

9. A clear warning sign of dangerous conversation is when you leave feeling devalued and unappreciated.

10. Controlling people are often hurting people who long to regain emotional balance in their lives.

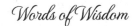

Words of Wisdom

A friend loves at all times, and kinsfolk are born to share adversity.

—Proverbs 17:17

Power Quote

When right people enter your life, right things begin to happen.

—Mike Murdock

Plan of Action

Relationships are like teeter-totters with two people on opposite sides struggling to establish a healthy balance between the ups and downs of life. The healthiest relationships are those that support a mutual flow of contribution and commitment. Take time to reflect on your relationships. Write a note of encouragement to those who need it most and remember to honor those who have shaped your life in a positive way.

— 5 —

Green-Eyed Monsters

Happiness is having a dream you cannot let go
of and a partner who would never ask you to.

—Robert Brault

I remember feeling my heart shatter into a million tiny pieces. I was thoroughly convinced my broken heart would never fully recover, and trying to convince me otherwise would have been a colossal waste of energy. It was years before I discovered the breakup with my ex-boyfriend did not shatter my heart; it simply revealed the underlying truth. My heart had never been whole.

The relationship had been more unbalanced than I dared believe. It took months of wrestling with the truth, excruciating anguish, and serious introspection to face facts. My insecurities were the primary source of our incompatibility. My ex-boyfriend was forced to juggle many roles, including life coach, spiritual leader, therapist, BFF, personal cheerleader, and love interest, as he tried to fill the emotional vacuums in my life. The problem was I needed more time and attention than one man could provide. The barebones truth of the matter is I found it difficult to receive love because I felt unworthy of being loved.

First-Rate Heartbreak

A dear friend shared with me his private struggle to prolong a relationship with a woman who suddenly ended their yearlong romance. In an anguished tone he divulged his heartbreak:

> I can honestly say I did everything imaginable to express love to my fiancée. Lavishing her with gifts, supporting her dreams, and constantly verbalizing my love for her left me totally unprepared to receive the news that she was calling off our engagement. For weeks she ignored my phone calls, and I spent sleepless nights wondering where and how our relationship went wrong. When she finally agreed to meet me for coffee, I asked her to explain her sudden decision. Her response left me stunned. She said, "I constantly struggled to feel worthy of your love. I thought you deserved someone better, so I broke off our relationship." My heart sank. What did she mean by "feeling unworthy of my love"? Once more I tried to affirm my love for her. I have never heard from her again.

If you have been traumatized by a relationship ending unexpectedly, be assured you are not alone. Millions of people have found themselves in the dramatic backlash of a broken relationship. Separation, a parting of ways, a split: however you want to label it, rejection from a relationship gone wrong still hurts.

What I have noticed is no one seems to handle the heartbreak of rejection in exactly the same way. Although similar in experience, breakups vary in intensity. Consider Bethany, who was back into the dating scene less than a month after discovering her boyfriend was cheating on her with her best friend. Then there is Kyle. He became engaged six months after a disastrous three-year romance ended. But not all hearts recover so quickly. I remember another friend, Marshall, who was not as fortunate. After years of collecting the pieces to his broken heart, he decided to spend the rest of his life in seclusion. A few weeks ago, I watched a successful forty-year-old drive himself to the brink of insanity because the woman he was dating decided to break off their three-month-long relationship. For some, a broken relationship spells the end of all romantic interests. Rejection serves as a nail in relationship's coffin. Others express little if any grief. What is the defining difference? Is one person simply stronger than another? Do some people love with less intensity? Or has one group simply discovered a more balanced outlook on love and rejection? Below I address the top five relationship questions that flood my inbox.

1. How do you get over someone you love when they do not feel the same way?

This question proves one of the most challenging. Being in love with someone who doesn't feel the same way is not a problem you fix but one you must work through. The first step in the right direction is to recognize that rejection is your private conductor leading you to healthy, successful relationships. As I stated earlier, one of the benefits of rejection is that it alerts you to wrong people who may not qualify for your future.

One thing I have learned is, people do not have the same capacity for love. What do I mean? Perhaps the best way to explain is to distinguish the difference between ability and capacity. According to *Merriam-Webster's Dictionary*, the word *ability* means natural aptitude; the state of being able; the physical, mental, or legal power to perform.[1] It also defines the word *capacity* as the potential or suitability for holding, storing, or accommodating.[2] The God-given ability to love is limitless. The capacity to give and receive love is a condition of our relationship with God, past experiences, and relationships.

But human love has its limitations. If we could calculate the ability to love in terms of measurement, some people could fill a milk jug with love, others a swimming pool, and still others could fill an ocean. Why is this true? Because not everyone exercises their God-given ability to love or be loved. This principle is important for you to understand. If you are in a dating relationship with someone who is incapable or unwilling to return love, it is to your benefit to release them. Release them into their future so you can walk into yours. There is someone—I speculate to say, more than one—who will be head-over-heels in love with you. The key is refusing to settle for less than God's best for your life. Chances are those who are incapable of discerning your personal worth today stand little chance of discerning it tomorrow. Wait for the one who will recognize and celebrate your individuality. Remember, it is not about getting over a person or convincing them to love you; it is about discerning the right person God has designed for you.

2. How do I keep damaged relationships from the past from becoming the relationship template of my future?

First loves are unforgettable. This is especially true of first loves ending tragically. We all have reasons for stubbornly holding on to our first starry-eyed relationships. Some subconsciously bookmark a time when romantic love is first awakened. Others remember just how sharp an arrow Cupid's bow shoots. Whatever the list of reasons for memorializing those early relationships, we must guard our hearts to ensure the pain of youthful or inexperienced love does not negatively impact our future relationships. Grace's story is an excellent example of how experiencing a bitter relationship at a young age can form defective or flawed patterns for future relationships:

> Matt was my first love. He was my boyfriend, high-school crush, and senior prom date. I remember all too well the

extravagant dress my father paid a small fortune for and the excitement I felt leading up to Friday night's dance. My emotions were high and my heart totally unprepared for the pain that was to follow.

Can you imagine the rejection I felt, arriving at the dance only to watch Matt flirt and dance with every other girl in the room? Crushed, embarrassed, mad, and confused, I questioned what was wrong with me. Was I not pretty enough? Did my breath smell? Did I look like a freak dancing? Three-quarters of the way through the dance I left with a friend in a full-blown rage. To make matters worse, the next day I found out Matt had taken another girl home and had sex with her. My outlook on love and relationships was forever tainted. This crushing encounter with my first love set the tone for decades of wrong decisions. Thoroughly convinced all men were unreliable, liars, cheaters, and only out for sex, I expected nothing less in future relationships—and that is exactly what I experienced.

A similar story may have happened to you. It may not have occurred at your prom, but somewhere in your past, a negative relationship experience formed your expectations for future relationships. Although rejection is unavoidable, how it affects future relationships is entirely your decision. Rejection is like a two-sided coin, with one side branded "bitter" and the other side stamped "better." Only you can decide if the fingerprints of rejection will leave trace marks of pain or lead you to a higher purpose.

Like photos on a time line, rejection is a proven memory maker. The memories you call to mind most often give shape to future thoughts and actions. A constant stream of negative memories is similar to pouring blood into a shark tank. It attracts hungry predators who seek to consume the broken and bleeding. I use this illustration to emphasize that negative thoughts breed negative reactions. If your goal is to prevent wrong relationships from affecting future relationships, you must rinse away the bitter aftertaste of relationships gone wrong from your thought life.

3. What part, if any, do parental relationships play in romantic relationships?

Andrew was in a long-term relationship with a lovely, outgoing young woman named Jillian. Raised in an affluent family by parents happily married for thirty-five years, she thrived. Andrew, however, brought up in a single-parent home by a mother who had met with her share of broken relationships, suffered from self-esteem issues. Andrew was the focus of his mother's world. In her eyes, he was the image of perfection and the only dependable man in the world. Need I say more? If you have lived this nightmare you know the direction I am going.

Convinced Jillian was the devil in a dress, Andrew's mother used underhanded, if not outright devious tactics to plant seeds of dissention into their relationship. As you can imagine, when Andrew announced his plans to marry

Jillian, his mother flew into a rage. Trying her best to convince Andrew that Jillian was spoiled, idealistic, out of touch with reality, and not the right choice for him, she told him he needed to find a "hard-working, down-to-earth" kind of wife. Tainted by the strong influence of his mother, Andrew and Jillian's relationship suffered.

A parent's attitude toward the opposite sex plays a large role in his or her child's ability to develop healthy relationships. If a mother portrays a negative attitude toward men, in all likelihood, her son will develop a negative attitude toward women.[3] Like the raging waters of Niagara Falls, the wounds of rejection can easily spill over into the next generation. In the above scenario, Andrew's mother's feelings of rejection not only influenced her own relationships but also Andrew's. Experiencing firsthand his mother's bitterness toward men led him to assume all women felt bitterness toward men. Her negative experiences and reluctance to release her feelings of rejection adversely affected Andrew's ability to have a healthy relationship with Jillian.

Rejection can sneak into our lives through people we wouldn't suspect and circumstances we cannot control. Rejection doesn't wait for us to open the door or send out engraved invitations; it simply walks right in. Because of rejection's total disregard for boundaries, I want to empower you with ways you can experience the euphoria of healthy and happy relationships. Following are a few empowerment tips I want you to remember:

1. Never allow a dysfunctional relationship to become the benchmark or guide for future relationships.
2. Resist the temptation to carry damaged emotions of one relationship into a future relationship.
3. Guard your heart against negative perceptions of the opposite sex.
4. Discern the influence parental rejection plays in your relationships.
5. Recognize how parental attitudes shape your self-image.

One thing is for certain: God never intended relationships to be a source of pain. Instead, relationships were created as a source of pleasure. In our guidebook, the Bible, God clearly outlines His purpose for uniting a man and woman. He joins them together for the divine purpose of enjoyment, companionship, and fulfilling their assignments on earth.

4. My spouse often flies into a jealous rage. Is this type of behavior normal or healthy?

If you have ever played a game of charades then you will understand the analogy I am about to make. A *charade* is a term meaning, "to act out or pantomime." A game of charades is played by dividing members into teams. Each team is then given the opportunity to act out key words, titles, or characters. The team that guesses the most pantomimes correctly is declared the winner. How does jealousy apply to a game of charades? That's easy. Jealousy acts as a charade, mimicking or impersonating an unbroken heart.

Imagine a little girl playing dress-up. Envision her in her mother's closet, wrapped in a chiffon scarf, draped in layers of costume jewelry, and wearing a pair of red stilettos. She looks into the mirror and imagines she is her mother. But in reality, she is a five-year-old dressed in baggy clothes, gaudy jewelry, and oversized shoes. Jealousy does the same thing. It likes to play dress-up and pretend the issues of insecurity, anger, rage, suspicious thinking, or verbal accusations somehow mask a wounded heart. Whether it's a boy pretending to have the bravado of a man or a wounded fifty-year-old who misbehaves like a child, the truth is others see through the well-crafted disguise.

As a matter of fact, jealousy does more than reveal insecurity; it highlights insecurity. The mask intended for protection becomes a bull's-eye, a big red-and-black target painted on one's backside that says, "I'm a vulnerable, broken person with trust issues. Go ahead; shoot me while I'm not looking." Be assured, most of the time jealousy is simply playing dress-up and is actually insecurity.

Let's take an imaginary journey. Picture yourself walking through the mall, arm in arm with the man of your dreams. The day has been perfect—lunch at a five-star restaurant, shopping at your favorite store . . . until you turn the corner and run into his gorgeous ex-girlfriend. You try to smile, make small talk, and look unaffected by her presence, but inside you are fuming. The rest of the day is ruined as you inwardly rehash questions of insecurity: *Is he still thinking about her? Will she try to contact him? Do they still have feelings for each other? Did they spend time together at this mall? Did she look better than me today?* Similar scenarios happen daily. The most important thing you can ask yourself is: *How will I respond when faced with a situation that blows my insecurities out of the water? Will I create a scene in public and place blame on an innocent third party, or more forward with confidence? Remember, nothing screams insecurity move than a full-out jealous fit.*

To discover what drives someone to react in a jealous rage, we need to get out our shovels and dig down deep. Beneath what appears to be a crusty layer of bad manners and ill-temperament is a hidden truth. Jealousy is a response to fear, which is the root of all insecurity. Keep in mind, the top issues people wrestle with in life can be traced back to fear. The fear of losing something or someone they love will often prompt feelings of insecurity, manifesting as jealousy. For example, when you see the person you're romantically involved with talking to someone of the opposite sex, you may feel vulnerable or threatened. The overwhelming fear that they may develop feelings for another person may trigger unpredictable, even irrational thoughts. Thoughts are powerful. Repetitive thoughts, even fictional ones, if unchecked, can seem real—especially in the mind of the wounded. The mind can create a make-believe masterpiece in a matter of moments.

Believe it or not, there are people who enjoy it when

their love interest acts jealous. I once had a close friend explain it this way:

> I like it when another man looks at me with special interest or says something flirtatious in front of my husband. Although it makes him angry, it makes me feel good. His jealous reactions prove he feels I am worth fighting for.

Sadly, the only time my friend feels significant to her husband is when another man makes him feel threatened or insecure. Yes, we know men are less verbal than women and often have a difficult time expressing feelings of love and commitment. But trust me when I tell you, there are more creative ways to gain affirmation than provoking your significant other to respond with jealousy. If your romantic interest hasn't learned to express his feelings verbally or in the way you would most enjoy, offer suggestions, key phrases or words you would enjoy hearing. But stop provoking the person you love to jealousy; it will produce anger, not affection.

Are you catching on to the fact that jealousy reveals insecurity? By purposefully provoking someone to become jealous, you promote their weaknesses and reveal their insecurities. This type of behavior is inexcusable. Remember, healthy relationships flourish when nurtured by mutual trust and security, not fear.

Healthy relationships flourish when nurtured by mutual trust and security, not fear.

Jealous accusations are not isolated to romantic relationships. They occur in professional relationships and friendships and are often the fuel for family feuds. Let's take a quick quiz and assess how jealousy and insecurity could be affecting your life.

The Green-Eyed Monster Quiz

1. Do you have to work hard to celebrate the success of others?
2. When you visit the home of friends who are more affluent, do you leave feeling like a failure?
3. Do you often feel your friends and coworkers seem to have a better life than you?
4. Do your friends or spouse often accuse you of being jealous?
5. Do you feel energized, special, or secure when others seem envious of your success?
6. During the holidays do you get the impression other family members receive preferential treatment or excessive amounts of attention?

How did you do? Did you respond yes to three or more questions? If so, I suspect you are fighting the green-eyed monsters known as jealousy and insecurity.

Taming the Monsters

A young man once asked me, "How do I control the unexplainable rage I feel when I see my girlfriend talking to another guy? Is there a cure for my jealousy?" My response was both yes and no. As I explained earlier, jealousy is a response, a reaction to the deeper issue of insecurity. Please understand that it is virtually impossible to tame a green-eyed monster without experiencing healing from insecurity. Healing is the key that locks away the monster of insecurity once and for all. But before we lock this monster away, he must first be tamed. How do you tame something as wild and unruly as jealousy? It is easier than you might imagine. Let's begin with the basics.

The first step is to recognize jealous feelings are reflective of negative self-imagery. Jealousy magnifies the fear that our flaws disqualify us from love. The fact is, when real love is involved, nothing could be further from the truth. Love extends beyond our greatest weaknesses and obvious failures. The second step is to meet jealous thoughts or reactions head-on. Begin countering any negative thoughts or words with positive affirmation. For example, when tempted to believe your life is worthless and you are an inconvenience to others, take this opportunity to remind yourself that friends and family members choose to be a part of your life because they genuinely love and care about you. Second Corinthians 10:5 reminds us to confront our thoughts, bringing them into captivity and obedience unto Christ.

One of the greatest ways to conquer jealousy is to ask, "Is there a logical reason for my jealous actions, or am I displaying my insecurities for the world to see?" Sometimes we need to do ourselves a favor and put away the flashlight that spotlights our insecurities. Above all, stop the comparison game. God created only one you. That means you are irreplaceable. You are priceless in His sight and are more valuable than you will ever know.

When dealing with rejection, remember to view past experiences through the lens of God's love and grace. The truth is, you have been fearfully and wonderfully created by a loving God. You were not an acci-

> When dealing with rejection, remember to view past experiences through the lens of God's love and grace.

dent or afterthought. In Jeremiah 1:5 God describes His thoughts toward you: "Before I formed you in the womb I knew you, and before you were born I consecrated you." God loves you with an everlasting love and delights in speaking blessings over your life. If you have struggled to know or understand the infinite love of your heavenly Father then I invite you to read His words of comfort, hope, and healing.

5. I have the feeling my girlfriend enjoys playing mind games with me. Should I play along or is it okay to simply say no?

At the core of every strong relationship is healthy communication. Healthy communication includes learning that how you disagree is often more important than why you disagree. Disagreements happen, opinions differ, but arguments should not center on accusation. Let's consider the enraged husband who shouts at his wife, "Go ahead and leave; I know you want to!" or "Why don't you run off with your boss? The two of you seem to work really well together." Accusing his wife is an unhealthy way of trying to discover her feelings without expressing his insecurities. Many people who find it difficult to put their feelings into words use accusatory statements during arguments. Let me be loud and clear: it should not take an argument to get to the bottom of what casual conversation has kept concealed. There are more effective ways to communicate doubt, concern, or fear. One doesn't have to have a genius-level IQ to convey feelings in an honest, clear-cut way. The first step toward building successful and long-lasting relationships is to toss aside the mind games and get back to the brass tacks of honesty.

There are many mixed messages about how a person should feel in a relationship, especially a romantic relationship. A few hours spent watching afternoon talk shows will create lingering doubts if not outright confusion when it comes to relationship advice. While one side argues how complicated and demanding relationships are, the other side implies that if you are lucky enough to discover and marry your soul mate everything will end happily ever after. The balanced truth is, strong relationships are not discovered but fostered

> If you long to feel secure in a relationship you must begin by feeling secure with yourself.

and carefully maintained. If you long to feel secure in a relationship you must begin by feeling secure with yourself. Confidence plays an important role in building strong, balanced relationships. Relationships with high levels of communication, trust, and a mutual freedom to express open and honest feelings are usually the strongest and most lasting. Learning to feel secure before you enter a romantic relationship will guarantee a strengthened mutual relationship.

Chapter Principles

1. Rejection is your private conductor leading you to healthy, successful relationships.

2. Chances are, those who are incapable of discerning your personal worth today stand little chance of discerning it tomorrow.

3. Rejection is like a two-sided coin: one side branded "bitter" and the other side stamped "better."

4. Like photos on a time line, rejection is a proven memory maker. The memories you call to mind most often give shape to future thoughts and actions.

5. A parent's attitude toward the opposite sex plays a large role in his or her child's ability to develop healthy relationships with the opposite sex. If a mother portrays a negative attitude toward men, in all likelihood, her son will develop a negative attitude toward women.

6. Rejection doesn't wait for us to open the door or to send out engraved invitations. It simply walks right in.

7. Jealousy acts as a charade, mimicking or impersonating a rejected heart.

8. Jealousy does more than reveal insecurity; it highlights insecurity.

9. Jealousy is not an *emotion,* but rather a strong *reaction* to feelings of insecurity. Jealousy is a response to fear, which is the root of all insecurity.

10. Thoughts are powerful. Repetitive thoughts, even fictional ones, if unchecked, can seem real—especially in the mind of the wounded.

Words of Wisdom

All the words of my mouth are righteous; there is nothing twisted or crooked in them.

—PROVERBS 8:8

Power Quote

Love doesn't hurt; loving the wrong person does.

—UNKNOWN

Plan of Action

The *Merriam-Webster's Dictionary* defines *friend* as, "A person whom one knows, likes, and trusts; a person with whom one is allied in a struggle or cause; comrade; one who supports."[4] Everyone has three emotional needs: acceptance, understanding, and affirmation. When those needs are met, relationships thrive. Remember to take time to check your relationships. They are one of the greatest investments in your life.

Families and Fudge

*Call it a clan, call it a network, call
it a tribe, call it a family.
Whatever you call it, whoever
you are, you need one.*

—JANE HOWARD

Someone once said, "Families are like fudge—mostly sweet with a few nuts." Although I laugh at this statement, I daresay that is exactly the dynamic of most families. Splintered and fragmented, today's family tree looks more like a twisted vine than a deeply rooted elm. Family dysfunction has become the modern-day catchphrase representing the condition of many American homes. What was once a refuge from the raging waters of rejection has become a source of rejection. Therein lies our dilemma. How do we

Dysfunctional patterns of rejection within the family must stop.

stop the self-inflicted blows of rejection? Before we tackle that question, let's focus on one point: dysfunctional patterns of rejection within the family must stop. Do you agree? With a positive and ready-to-learn mind-set, it is time to dive headlong into a sea of solutions.

PINPOINTING THE POISON

It is impossible to discover a cure without first pinpointing the poison. In exactly the same way, to stop the toxic flow of rejection, you must first discover its source.

Toxins are man-made poisons that can only be produced by other living substances. Synthetic or unnatural sources are powerless to manufacture these unhealthy contaminants. Where am I going with this? I want to remind you, rejection, like any toxin, remains powerless until connected with a living entity. It cannot be transferred to something or someone who is unwilling to host its toxicity. How then do you keep the toxin of rejection from negatively affecting your life? What safeguards are necessary to keep rejection from oozing into the delicate fabric of your family? You can begin by identifying factors that trigger feelings of rejection. Let's look at a few.

SIBLING RIVALRY

Amy is a perfect example of how rejection plays into the complexity of family dynamics. The eldest of four and the only child by a different father, her story is documented below.

My childhood remains stained by painful memories of rejection. The truth is I have never felt accepted by my family. Growing up, my mother was unquestionably partial to my siblings. For every gift I received they received two. Even today, if you were to walk through my mother's home you would notice many pictures of my siblings but very few of me. Although my sisters and I are on the same social networking sites they only list each other as siblings. I rarely receive pictures of my nieces or nephews although I faithfully send them pictures of our children. It is difficult for me to wrap my mind around such obvious rejection. For years I blamed myself for their actions. Trust me. Self-blame is easy to do when you are the target of family hostility.

Amy is not alone in the battle for acceptance. Unfortunately, when it comes to rejection, her story proves the standard, not the exception.

The Faux Pas of Favoritism

If a biblical list of parental blunders and faux pas were created, favoritism would top the list. Imagine the Old Testament scene as Joseph's father presented him with the coat of many colors. If any of his eleven brothers had lingering doubts about Jacob's partiality they were now put to rest. One act . . . one coat . . . the father's favoritism revealed and on display. One has to question, what was this father thinking? It is doubtful that Jacob was thinking; more likely he was imitating the behavior patterns of his parents. Parental favoritism, which virtually shattered Jacob's own childhood, was about to destroy his sons. Had he not learned the dangers of preferential treatment? Why was he repeating family failures? The same reason many do. We unconsciously imitate the same destructive relationship patterns we observe during childhood. Statistically, what we witness in childhood we generally model in adulthood. If you have experienced failure in creating strong and healthy relationships, I sincerely recommend reviewing the relationship principles modeled before you as a child. Take time to consider the parental style of your parents. Are you mimicking wrong parental attitudes, or worse, weaving them into the lives of your children?

Out of all relationships, perhaps the parent-child relationship is the most fragile and complex. Therefore, I want to teach you how to effectively survive what I call the parent trap. You know the balancing act of expressing care without smothering, being lenient yet not condoning wrong behavior. Below are a few tips that will help you build strong, balanced parental relationships.

Keep Crisis from Becoming a Career

Some parents thrive on the dysfunctional behavior of their children. Why? It makes them feel emotionally connected and validated. Becoming overly involved in the life of your child is an easy trap to fall into, but it can create an unhealthy or codependent relationship. Consider the five-year-old boy who falls off his bike and cries for the attention of his mother. He panics, and she rushes to his rescue. What a beautiful example of love and trust when you are five. The same scenario is not so appealing at twenty-five. It is important for parents to identify which bump in the road calls for a Band-Aid and which qualifies for an ambulance. The difference in loving someone and needing their approval is profound. Let me give you another example.

Growing up, Cody was smart, handsome, and charming enough to sell cookies to a girl scout. Serving two jail sentences for theft and fraud, he turned out to be the nicest loser you would ever want to meet. What happened? Were his parents unloving? Did he have an unstable childhood? No, in fact, his parents were loving, forgiving, and compassionate. They were also enablers. As a boy, his mother caught him stealing from her purse. He smiled and told a smooth lie, and she believed him. Cody had a need for attention, and his mother had a need to be needed. With a lengthy list of financial catastrophes, divorces, and lawsuits, he made crisis his lifelong career. Unfortunately his life continued to spiral out of control. His parents were left in financial ruin and his children grew up without a father. Could these circumstances have been averted? With time, love, and a healthy dose of discipline, yes. Remember, love does not grant permission to do wrong. It restrains so one can reap the rewards of doing right. As we are about to see, love and approval are not the same.

CONFRONT WHEN NECESSARY

The biblical account of 2 Samuel 11 reads like a modern-day tabloid.

Scandal surrounds politician accused of
adultery, love child, and murder.

King David had committed adultery with Bathsheba, the wife of Uriah. When Bathsheba revealed she was pregnant with his child, David arranged to murder Uriah. He plotted. He covered. He deceived. He did what all liars do; he lied more. Many parents would have made excuses, evaded questions, or enabled their child's actions. Not God. God doesn't play favorites. He did what any loving parent should do: He gave David time to repent and then confronted David's sin. God's love and mercy addressed his issues for the purpose of setting David free from the bondage of sin. Confrontation led to freedom and joy, which only come through repentance.

Take a moment and examine your heart. Has the fear of rejection kept you from confronting issues when family is involved? Do you withhold correction for fear others will withhold their love or affection? Parents are not the only ones who avoid arguments.

My friend Nicole faces confrontation on a different level. Her husband, an extremely successful lawyer, is a closet alcoholic. Because he provides a good income and a beautiful home and is the father of their two children, she evades facts to avoid confrontation. After all, his children adore him, colleagues idolize him, and people enjoy his company. Is the chaos that accompanies conflict really worth addressing his battle with alcoholism? What if she challenges his addiction and he files for divorce? Perhaps only she is qualified to answer these intimate questions. But one thing is for certain: things rarely change without confrontation. Yes, the dreaded word: *confrontation*. Before you stop reading, allow me to clarify that statement. For many, the word *confrontation* brings to mind a room of disgruntled and bitter relatives dredging up past failures and shouting angry insults. While that may be typical of many interventions, those are not the type I am referring to. What I am talking about are positive and constructive ways to address difficult if not excruciating situations.

> One thing is for certain: things rarely change without confrontation.

When someone you love is acting in a harmful or self-destructive manner, it is normal to want to take action that may prevent the behavior from worsening. The key is to carefully examine your motives for intervention. If your heart is in the right place, make certain your actions are equally well thought out. Creating a well-designed and positive intervention is a must. If confrontation remains an option, remember the following guidelines:

- *Address current actions of bad behavior.* It is pointless to dredge up twenty years' worth of toxic behavior. Stick to the crisis at hand. How are they behaving today? Specifically, how are their actions impacting your relationship?

- *Carefully lay out the facts.* Resist the urge to discuss speculations or hearsay. Make sure to use singular, not plural, terminology to express a personal opinion. For instance, instead of saying, "Everyone knows," say, "I know." Replace generic statements of "We all feel" with "When you come home drunk, I feel . . ." Speaking in a calm, loving voice will convey right intention.

- *Stay focused.* A person suffering from addiction or acting out in rebellion will be quick to change or manipulate the topic at hand. Keep on track; stick to the subject. Refuse to be pulled into needless arguments or discussions that distract from the issue.

- *Keep emotions from escalating.* Although you may not agree with a person's actions, be willing to listen to how they are feeling. Give them time to express why they do what they do. This will give you a clearer understanding of their motives and intentions.

- *Close the conversation by painting a picture of a positive tomorrow.* Focus on reasonable solutions and answers. There is more to an intervention than listing problems and complaints. Come to the negotiating table prepared to construct an optimistic future.

Confrontations can be complicated. At times you may feel like a trapeze artist, fighting to maintain balance while walking a very thin line. The key is to stay focused and remember the objective. With the right attitude and plan, a confrontation can turn the tables on dysfunction.

PREVENT THE STING

When I think about the effects of stubbornness, my mind races back to a story my Sunday school teacher shared about a little girl named Carole. The daughter of an affluent and well-respected couple in Chicago, Carole had parents who provided her the best education, tutors, and private lessons money could buy. Her nannies were given strict orders: "Whatever Carole wants, she can have; nothing is off-limits to our precious girl." While walking through the garden one day, Carole spotted a beautiful yellow flower. "Look!" she shrieked. "Flower! I want the flower!" The nanny gently shook her head and said, "No, honey, the flower will hurt you." The more she protested, the more Carole demanded. From a corner window of the house, Carole's mother scolded the nanny, "I told you, whatever she wants, she can have." With a disbelieving nod, the nanny let Carole reach for the flower. She squeezed it tightly and then screamed with pain, for inside the flower was a bright yellow bumble bee. Thirty years later, I still remember the moral of this story: many will give you what you want, but true love will guard you from what you do not need.

Can you relate to Carole? Is your life a mess because you refused to listen to the wisdom of someone who perceived dangerous pitfalls you ignored? Could tragedy have been prevented by yielding to the caution light of good judgment or sound reasoning? Why is it difficult to take correction? Could it be most people have trouble differentiating between correction and rejection?

A person who struggles with deep-rooted rejection issues may find it difficult to receive correction in a positive light. Those who have battled through the trenches of insecurity know all too well the anxiety associated with correction. It is an easy step to misconstrue correction as a personal attack on their character. Emotionally the struggle to separate someone's evaluation of their work from his evaluation of them as a person becomes larger than life. The deeper the rejection the harder it becomes for the mind not to misinterpret correction as rejection. A heart wounded by rejection will typically recoil at the slightest inference their efforts, job skills, or abilities are less than adequate. Let's examine this issue more closely.

Billy is a superstar on the baseball field. His pitching stats are through the roof and his batting average is almost double his teammates'. However, when his pitching coach makes a casual suggestion about correcting his three-finger grip curve ball, he withdraws and remains despondent for days.

How about Michelle, whose culinary skills won her a spot on a local food network? An immense success, her show is nominated for an award after its second season. Many given the same opportunity would be ecstatic. Not Michelle. She spends days sulking over a handful of negative e-mails from viewers. That's what rejection, left unconfronted, has the potential to do. It will train the mind to misinterpret a critique of *what I am doing* and replace it with *the person I am becoming*. Learning to differentiate personal evaluation and the evaluation of one's work is crucial. One day, wrestling with issues of rejection and correction, I stumbled upon an enlightening passage I want to share with you:

> The Lord disciplines the one he loves, and he chastens everyone he accepts as his son. Endure hardship as discipline; God is treating you as his children. For what children are not disciplined by their father? If you are not disciplined—and everyone undergoes discipline—then you are not legitimate, not true sons and daughters at all. (Hebrews 12:6–8 NIV)

Wow. These verses offer a welcoming outlook on correction. God makes it clear: correction proves He loves and accepts us as His children. Let that principle sink into your spirit. In order to turn the tables on rejection, it is vital we interpret correction as love and not rejection. Does everyone who critiques or censures your work have good intentions? Of course not. Admittedly, there are power-hungry egomaniacs who do not have your best interest at heart. But most of the time, those who care enough to give you positive feedback genuinely care about your life and future. Again,

God makes it clear: correction proves He loves and accepts us as His children.

the key to working rejection for your benefit is to consider its source and treat feedback as an invaluable resource.

KNOW WHEN TO CUT THE CORD

It can be difficult for parents to accept that their precious little one has developed into a full-grown adult. If you are independent and living on your own, it is past time to cut the umbilical cord. There is nothing more unattractive to a woman than a man whose relationship with his mother is clingy and needy. If you have started a family, make a mental note not to become a *helicopter parent*. What is a helicopter parent? A parent who lingers close by, waiting to swoop down and intervene in the child's life when needed.[1]

Is it wrong to be supportive or available to your kids? No, but maintaining a healthy balance is key. Keep in mind, an overly protective parent can inadvertently keep children from learning valuable life lessons that will develop them into strong and independent adults. This can produce dysfunctional behavior in both the parent and child. Consider the analogy below and highlight the symptoms stemming from an excessive and dependent relationship.

Rarely seen without the other, Marsha and Tyra acted more like sisters then mother and daughter. They shopped together, purchased the same type of car, and wore the same designer-label clothing. You may be wondering, what is wrong with that? Isn't it common for families to share the same interests or purchase similar items? Yes, but not to the extreme of those bound in codependent relation-ships. Signs of unhealthy bonding began to surface when Tyra broke up with her long-term boyfriend Billy and then insisted her mother break off her relationship with Jessie, her fiancée. More troubling was Tyra's bout with alcohol and her mother's need to take care of her unending list of demands. Their days are spent at the neighborhood bar or alone in their two-bedroom apartment. Codependent, they remain bound together by the fear of rejection.

Simply defined, codependency is the need to hold on to a relationship even when it is unhealthy. Perhaps the best way to convey the meaning of codependency is to share some of its defining characteristics. Here are a few examples to better explain:

- A codependent person may abandon his or her friends, place a career on hold, or compromise core beliefs to accommodate the desires of a partner.
- A codependent person feels responsible for the behavior or reactions of another.
- A codependent person will mirror the emotional responses of others.
- A codependent person exhibits extreme caretaking syndrome.
- A codependent person feels guilty exercising his or her individuality.
- A codependent person feels anxious when separated from his or her partner even for a short time.

- A codependent person needs approval from a partner before making decisions.
- A codependent person often exhibits other addictive behaviors.

Why have I taken time to discuss the issue of codependency? Because I have walked arm in arm with rejection. I am all too familiar with the underlying fear that questions, "Is there anyone who loves me enough to take care of me?" I have witnessed the agony of those who spend their lives looking for someone to take care of them only to end up a caretaker to others. I have also watched dozens of people just like Marsha and Tyra remain trapped in another's world, too afraid to live in their own. For these and other obvious reasons, codependent relationships are extremely unhealthy.

SUPERGLUE RELATIONSHIPS

What creates the crisis of codependency? Many factors, including the fear of abandonment or yearning for acceptance, can contribute to the excessive need of attachment to another. To get to the heart of the problem, let's examine some real-life scenarios.

Lori shares her story:

As a young teen my sister, Piper, became addicted to drugs. Our parents, who had issues of their own, were clueless on how to deal with an out-of-control, drug-addicted teen. Our father used physical force to try controlling her and our mother recoiled into a shell of denial. Eventually my father left home and I soon followed. My mother, unwilling to suffer more loss, spent the next twenty years at Piper's side, responding to her every whim and request. Her life is absorbed by my sister's addiction and codependent behavior.

Jason was affectionately referred to by his friends as "the army brat." After living in more than thirteen states in seventeen years, Jason's perception of stability was anything but typical. Rigid and stern, his father taught him emotions are superfluous and unnecessary. His idea of masculinity was to avoid any emotional interaction. It is common for children who are raised in a home where emotional response is discouraged to form codependent relationships as adults. The need to verbalize and express unguarded emotional feelings becomes overwhelming.

> You can spend your entire life trying to keep the love of others. But God's love is the only perfect love you will ever discover.

Codependent relationships simply do not work. Someone always ends up holding the short end of the stick. When we are tossed a line that somewhere out there is someone who completes us, we believe it. Perhaps that is the reason so many stay frustrated and leap from relationship to relationship. No one person has everything you need to complete you. A loving spouse can fulfill many of your longings and desires. But the plain truth is there remains a void in each of us only God's love and mercy can fulfill. There is a chamber within every heart that God reserves entirely for Himself. Money, fame, career, sex, and people cannot fill the space hallowed out by His hand. You can spend your entire life trying to keep the love of others. But God's love is the only perfect love you will ever discover.

"So we know and rely on the love God has for us. God is love. Whoever lives in love lives in God, and God in them" (1 John 4:16 NIV).

FIXERS

Different homes produce different types of dysfunction. Children who grow up feeling rejected will generally respond in one of two ways. They will either try to escape rejection or fix underlying causes associated with rejection. Let's deal with the fixers first.

Deanna grew up with a workaholic father and an alcoholic mother. Every day she rushed home from school to clean the house, cook a meal, and try to sober up her mother before her father walked through the front door. She thought if she could fix everything before her father came home, everything would be all right.

Fix the family. Fix the crisis at work. Fix it when friends get into a feud. Fix the lady's flat tire on the road. Fix the friend who doesn't have good personal style. Fix the neighbor's yard. Fix . . . fix . . . fix it or fail trying. Fixers are brilliant problem solvers and excellent employees. Unwilling to let a problem go unresolved, they stay with a task until completion. The downside to being a fixer is they are extreme people-pleasers. I know this firsthand.

I was a chronic fixer. I know the nature of the beast that seeks to please others to keep peace. The problem with fixers is we become toxic dump sites for those who are unwilling to deal with their emotional garbage. It took many years before I got the message: others are more than willing to let us walk through their manure heap as long as it keeps their feet clean. The need to please others makes us a target for others to trample through our lives and leave mounds of waste with no thought of regret. Is it any wonder we keep attracting controlling, abusive, codependent people into our lives? Truthfully, we don't have the energy or ability to make someone else happy. We can't love someone into being faithful. Faithfulness comes from character, not persuasion. Brass tacks? Regardless of how much we love them, we are incapable of talking alcoholics into sobriety. A girl can't turn enough cartwheels to make an unloving daddy notice her. She can't wear a skirt short enough to make a boy fall in love with her. There are not enough tricks in the book to win recognition from the unaccepting.

EVADERS

Seated in the center of his bed, Jackson maximized the volume of his headset while his parents went round two of a heated argument. He avoided confrontation like the plague. His parents' constant bickering and complaining made him want to pull the covers over his head and hide. The reality was neither headphones nor hiding would erase the hostility he felt at home.

That's the way it is when a huge elephant is in the middle of the room. Everyone can turn their heads, rearrange the furniture, step around the manure, and ignore it all they want, but the elephant is still there. Abusive relationships are no exception. We can dress up an elephant and pretend it's a coffee table, but others aren't fooled. Until we are willing to confront our issues, abusive cycles will not end.

Consider Braden, who told me:

I have finally come face-to-face with the truth. I am an easy target for the wrong kind of people. By dating women who only want my money and associating with friends who desire my influence, I have denied the truth. Now I see my actions and repetitive poor choices set me up for relationship failure. Sometimes people have difficulty believing the truth. I know; I can identify with delusion.

What is the remedy? How do we unravel the twisted knot of codependency? Work toward relational freedom one day at a time. Learn to avoid relationships that play on your insecurities. The more compassionate you are, the more likely others are to take advantage of your good-hearted nature. Rather than giving yourself quickly to others, take time to investigate their intentions. Give yourself gradually. Make sure a prospective relationship doesn't turn into a rejection-laden, codependent relationship.

Chapter Principles

1. Splintered and fragmented, today's family tree looks more like a twisted vine than a deeply rooted elm.

2. The home, which should be a refuge from the raging waters of rejection, has often become a source of rejection.

3. It is impossible to discover a cure without first pinpointing the poison. In order to stop the toxic flow of rejection, you must first discover its source.

4. Rejection, like any toxin, remains powerless until connected with a living entity.

5. The difference in loving someone and needing their approval is profound.

6. Love does not grant permission to do wrong but restrains so one can reap the reward of doing right.

7. Many will give you what you want, but true love will guard you from what you do not need.

8. A person experiencing ongoing feelings of rejection commonly perceives correction as a personal attack on his or her character.

9. The deeper the rejection the harder it becomes for the mind not to misinterpret correction as rejection.

10. The key to working rejection for your benefit is to consider its source and treat feedback as an invaluable resource.

<hr />

Words of Wisdom

Finally, all of you, have unity of spirit, sympathy, love for one another, a tender heart, and a humble mind.

—1 PETER 3:8

<hr />

Power Quote

I take rejection as someone blowing a bugle in my ear to wake me up and get going, rather than retreat.

—SYLVESTER STALLONE

<hr />

Plan of Action

Imagine shipping porcelain or fine china around the world. It would be foolish to think something so delicate would arrive safely unless it is securely wrapped and labeled "Fragile—handle with care." Relationships are no exception. They must be protected and handled with extreme care. Years ago I read a wonderful book entitled *What My Parents Did Right*.[2] It was a beautiful collection of stories written by successful women who attribute at least one positive life skill, attitude, or belief to their parents. I encourage you to take a moment and do the same. As children it is easy to point out what our parents did wrong while failing to remember the things they did right.

With this thought in mind, take out a sheet of paper and divide it in half. On the right side list the top five things you enjoyed most about your childhood. Now on the left side, list the top five things you least enjoyed about your childhood. Which memories did you envision first? How did they make you feel? Most important, are those images or experiences affecting your relationships today?

Truth, Lies, and Fairy Tales

You can close your eyes to the things you do
not want to see, but you cannot close your
heart to the things you do not want to feel.

—AUTHOR UNKNOWN

Do you know someone who lies for no apparent reason? I do. In fact, I could tell you disturbing stories of people who have lied or concealed facts because they are too lazy to tell the truth. Picture the face of a four-year-old smothered in chocolate icing. Now imagine his mother asking where the last piece of cake went. Hm, a difficult choice for a four-year-old. Does he tell the truth? Dare to lie? If he lies, will she believe him? Will the need to overcome shame or disappointment override his reluctance to tell the truth? Carefully weaving a web of dishonesty, he tells his mother what he believes she wants to hear—a story of convenience. Lies, however, are anything but convenient.

The Convenient Truth

I recently read a humorous online post by Dave McNeff, where he vividly describes the power of self-deception. Here is a modified version of the comical post:

> A blonde made several attempts to sell her old car. With the odometer nearing 340,000, she had trouble finding a buyer. She discussed the problem with a friend who suggested, "There may be a way to sell your car, but it's illegal." "That doesn't matter," replied the blonde. "All that matters is that I am able to sell this car." "All right," replied the friend. "Here is the address of a friend who owns a car repair shop around the corner. Tell him I sent you and he will turn the odometer on your car back to 40,000 miles. Then you will have no problem selling the car." Sure enough, the blonde went to the car repair shop as advised. About a month later her friend asked her, "Did you sell your car?" "No!" replied the blonde. "Why should I? It only has 40,000 miles on it."[1]

An illogical scenario, I know, but sometimes the greatest lies we believe are the one we tell ourselves. What makes a lie so enticing? Is it the comforting feeling of evading the consequences of our actions? Think about a time when you have been tempted to fabricate a lie. Was it when you felt inferior to others? Or, when you are in the presence of socially affluent friends, do you exaggerate your income or lifestyle? What about the infamous class reunion? Do you paint an elaborate self-portrait to gain the approval of others? Consider the wife who brags to her girlfriends about her perfect marriage yet goes home to a physically abusive husband. Men exaggerate their influence, women their relationships, young adults their bank accounts, sports figures lie about steroid use, and politicians make promises they never intend to keep.

Let's think about lying. Why does one reach for a lie when truth is as equally accessible? Is our human DNA wired to spin fallacious stories at the drop of a hat? Is it possible to avoid self-deception and speak only the bare facts? Let's explore the answers to these and other intriguing questions.

The Truth May Hurt, but a Lie Hurts More

If you have been given a promise only to have it taken back or left unfulfilled, you know the heartache that is certain to follow. Think about the father who promises to buy his son a new sports car for his sixteenth birthday but fails to deliver. Or the lady who convinced her friends and colleagues she was ten years younger than her actual age. Of course, when the truth came out, she was considered a laughingstock, and no one trusted her again. The reality is, people do not expect you to be superhuman. They do, however, expect you to be honest. Present the real you, let people know who you are upfront, and they will rarely be disappointed. Remember, others would rather be surprised by what you can do than be disappointed by what you claim to do. Sincerity and honesty will draw quality people toward, not away from, you.

The Original Fear Factor

What drives a person to lie or to evade the truth? One word: *fear.* The fear of consequences, failure, rejection, pain, or heartache makes deception seem like a candy-coated solution. Consider the infamous scene in the garden of Eden. What happened to God's perfect couple? Why did they partake of the forbidden fruit? Why were they forced to leave the perfect utopia called Eden? They believed a lie and willingly sinned. Believing a lie can be as damaging as telling one. Eve believed the lie of the serpent and Adam believed Eve. Buying into a lie led to sin and sin produced fear.

Let's examine the garden scene more closely. In Genesis 3:9–10, God peels back the foliage of garden shrubs and discovers Adam and Eve huddled together, trembling in fear. When God asked Adam why they were hiding, he explained that they hid in fear in response to His voice. And there you have it: the first man, the first woman, the first lie, the first sin, the first time a human experienced fear. What happens when you lie? You experience fear. Fear, the root of every untruth, jumps behind the first bush it can find and tells the first lie that comes to mind.

While telling a little white lie may seem harmless, it is actually an invitation, welcoming fear to invade your life. Deception is like a crouching lion. Waiting at the door and ready to pounce upon unsuspecting prey, it is an enemy we cannot ignore. When we lie, divert the truth, or act in a deceitful way, we crack open the door, providing predators the opportunity to create unnecessary chaos in our lives. If lies, untruth, and deceit are hinges that swing open the door to deception, then it stands to reason, truth is the lock that denies deception access. As we are about to discover, truth is an ally protecting us from unsuspecting enemies. Those enemies include the game-playing relationship junkie, the manipulative financial predator, and the emotional parasite, all of whom do not think twice about consuming your resources to meet their needs.

Players, Predators, and Parasites

Have you watched a good action movie recently? You know, two hours of nonstop, thrilling suspense. Imagine sitting on the edge of your seat, hanging on every word as you desperately try to distinguish the good guys from the bad guys. Years ago, producers simplified movie plots by dressing good guys in white and bad guys in black. Distinguishing the bad guys in real life, however, is not that simple.

I know a young woman who served time in prison for crimes she did not commit. This young woman's boyfriend convinced her if she truly loved him, she would serve out his prison sentence. Yes, shockingly, she believed him. Sometimes I seriously wonder how situations such as this happen. How can one's self-esteem be reduced to such depths? Why would an innocent person be willing to serve time in a federal penitentiary? Why do innocent people assume responsibility for the actions of villains? The more cases of injustice I study, the more I come to disdain manipulation. One thing I know: when an innocent party is willing to take the fall for actions they have not committed, it usually means they have experienced the heartbreaking pain of trusting a mind manipulator.

What Is Manipulation?

Manipulation is emotional extortion. It is the persuasive power to acquire from others what they do not want to give. Consider the friend or sibling who magically seems to get his or her way *no matter what*. These people have the uncanny way of persuading others to give them anything, sometimes everything, they desire. What's the trick? How does a tenant deliberately neglect to meet the obligations of his lease and then compel his proprietor to feel sorry, even apologetic, for expecting payment? By skillfully projecting emotions of self-pity and unworthiness onto his victim, he steals a trick right out of the con man's play book.

Persuading victims that they are, in fact, the villains, manipulators generate compassion from others, even when *they* are the ones inflicting pain. As you learn more about manipulation, remember two very important principles. First, a manipulator's primary pleasure is control. In the same way cocaine provides a euphoric high for an addict, control becomes an addictive high for a manipulator. Second, manipulators are polished liars. Since they fabricate stories that distort the truth, it will take a sharp mind and godly discernment to avoid the enticing words or actions of an experienced mind manipulator.

The correlation between rejection and manipulation is profound. In fact, the number one target for con artists and mind manipulators are those who have been emotionally wounded or rejected. I recently watched a documentary based on this very principle. The hour-long show brought to light the fact that a large percentage of scam artists search the Internet for bankruptcy or divorce notifications, even obituaries, to find their next victims. They target the vulnerable—specifically, the lonely, insecure, sick, or uneducated. Once they have identified their intended victims, the next step is to establish a relationship.

How does a villain befriend a victim? Manipulators gain the trust of their potential victims by portraying themselves as victims. After all, every hurting person longs for a friend who can understand his or her pain. The most destructive part of betrayal is that it undermines trust. Consider a time when you uncovered the evil schemes of a manipulator. How did you respond to the knife stuck in your back? Were you shocked? Disappointed? Did you question your ability to make wise decisions or to discern the motives of others?

Perhaps you were not swindled out of thousands of dollars, but you lost something greater: trust and self-respect. Feelings of doubt and shame are often hard to conquer, especially if you have been coerced into believing a lie.

If you have suffered from tragic feelings associated with betrayal, it is important for you to begin the healing journey toward wholeness. Healing begins by addressing the negative events that have taken place and then focusing on the positive takeaways that will help you be more discriminating in selecting who qualifies for your future.

Too Sweet

Have you ever met someone who seemed a little too sweet? You know who I am talking about. The person who always found ample time to talk through your problems and offer what appeared insightful wisdom on solving your crisis. Over time they gained your confidence, and dropping your emotional guard, you shared intimate secrets, personal information, or private stories. Then without warning, things changed and you discovered you had been maliciously deceived.

Is anyone genuinely prepared for the tidal waves of rejection and regret that follow bad decision-making? If you have experienced the emotional chaos of trusting a manipulative person, then you understand the fallout that is to come. The course of events usually follows this order: first there is the feeling of shock, which quickly turns to anger, then issues self-doubt, and finally self-loathing.

Questioning their ability to make quality decisions, the innocent turn inward and blame themselves for subscribing to the lies of a manipulator. Living in the ruins of another's reckless behavior, they not only took the bait but they now take the blame.

Sadly, similar scenarios happen more often than you think. What is the key to self-protection? Do we journey through life forming relationships and never trusting? Certainly not. Trust is the lifeline to every healthy relationship. The question is not *if* you should trust but rather who *qualifies* for your trust. Rejection can be avoided by discerning who belongs in your future.

If you have struggled to form strong, healthy, or long-lasting relationships, then it is time to reevaluate who qualifies for your future. You can learn how to detect and identify those who would manipulate your heart or mind for selfish gain. Remember, anyone who creates repetitive failure in your life does not belong in your future. Below I have listed several identifying signs a wrong person may be in your life. Please invest time to contemplate each one, asking God to reveal who belongs in your present and qualifies for your future.

CHARACTER TRAITS OF MANIPULATORS

- Manipulators are savvy. With sheer confidence they justify inappropriate behavior.

- Manipulators portray themselves as victims.
- A relationship with a manipulator becomes jeopardized the moment you refuse to follow their advice.
- The apology of a manipulator will be well-crafted and insincere.
- Manipulators methodically direct the course and direction of conversation.

Manipulators are like emotional fishermen. They are patient, shrewd, and calculating. Inside their tackle box is an assortment of hooks, bait, and lures designed to emotionally ensnare the big catch. One of the main baits manipulators use to reel in their victims is sympathy. Pretending to be victims, they use sympathy as a ploy to tug on the heartstrings of many well-meaning and caring people. Being expert liars, they fabricate stories of convenience, creating worlds that do not exist. In one brushstroke they exaggerate the truth, customizing their tale to those who will emotionally buy in. With a world full of game-players and manipulators, how are we to protect ourselves from their malicious strategies? I have listed the top six lies manipulators tell and the carefully crafted reasons why they tell them.

Top Six Lies Manipulators Tell

1. "I have never told anyone this before . . ." is the classic one-liner manipulators use to bridge trust.

Acting as if they are sharing highly personal information, they expect their victims to share intimate
details of their lives in return.

2. "You are the only person I really trust . . ." is a lie used
to create sympathy and compassion. It subtly communicates the message, *Although everyone else has
abandoned me, I believe you are different. I know you
will never betray my trust.* The goal of a manipulator
is to persuade others to pledge unfailing loyalty.

3. "You are the only *real person* I know . . ." is a craft-
ily designed lie portraying their victim as their only
source of trust. It is a sly way of compelling others
to be completely vulnerable and transparent.

4. "You are the only person I can relax and be my true
self around . . ." is a liar's slick shot at convincing others they are being open and honest. The aim is to
destroy any remaining walls of resistance or distrust.

5. "This is not about . . ." is every liar's favorite line.
If a manipulator becomes anxious or apprehensive
about a person's loyalty, they will plead the opposite of their true intent. For instance, if they stress
the point that the relationship is *not* about money,
be assured money is *exactly* their objective. It they
stress their motive is not to have a sexual relationship, be assured that is exactly what they have in
mind. Manipulators are notorious for expressing dis-
ingenuous motives to disarm their true objectives.

6. "I never want to see you get hurt" is a lie deferring

blame away from the perpetrator. The cruel truth is, they are warning their victim upfront, *This relationship will end tragically, but I will not take the blame.* This line is typically used when a manipulator feels the relationship is coming to an end.

Do any of these lies seem familiar? If we are truly honest, somewhere along the journey we have all taken the bait of an accomplished mind manipulator. I have been victimized by a chronic manipulator more than once. That is why I am passionate about sharing these principles with you. Rejection can often be avoided. Applying the wisdom others have discovered can safeguard our lives and those we love. Before closing this chapter, there are a few bonus takeaways I want to share with you.

When Good People Are Tempted to Lie

Are you ready for the truth? The best of God's people have succumbed to the temptation to lie. Consider Abraham, a man who carries illustrious titles as the father of faith, the friend of God, and the father of many nations. Could a righteous man like Abraham be vulnerable enough to lie? He was and he did. He instructed his wife, Sarah, to tell the men of Gerar she was his sister, not his wife (Genesis 20:1–2). Bound by the fear they would kill him to possess her, he pulled a fast one. He lied. In a matter of moments faith melted into a pool of fear.

Fear always challenges faith. Left unchecked, fear will manifest in lies and deceit. It is noteworthy enough for me to draw your attention to the fact that lying not only limits the blessings of God but it undermines reputations and credibility. When the men of Gerar discovered Abraham's untruthfulness, they addressed him as a liar instead of a man of faith. Good people may occasionally lie, but it is never without consequence. For every reason to lie there is a better reason not to lie. Remember, lies are told by those who are not creative enough to solve a problem with the truth. Show me an honest person and I will show you someone capable of solving life's toughest problems.

The good news is God never lies. One of the principal attributes differentiating God from man is His inability to tell a lie. Numbers 23:19 plainly states, "God is not a human being, that he should lie, or a mortal, that he should change his mind. Has he promised, and will he not do it? Has he spoken, and will he not fulfill it?" God is always honest—always.

The Rewards of Honesty

As a child I'm sure I heard "Honesty is always the best policy" more than a thousand times. It would take many painful experiences before I would understand the magnitude of this statement. Honesty *is* a policy. In the same way automobile insurance protects from unforeseen financial loss, the truth protects you from unanticipated emotional damage. The truth will defend and safeguard you from the careless or sometimes reckless actions of others. Just keep in mind, every policy has a premium. The premium for godly protection is honesty. God cannot defend dishonesty. If any part of your life is tainted by lies, covered in deceit, or you simply discover yourself being dishonest with God or others, repent. Get off the merry-go-round of deceit and begin a new journey toward freedom.

Sir Walter Scott said it best: "Oh what a tangled web we weave, when first we practice to deceive." What a powerful analogy. The word *web* is defined as "a network of fine threads used to ensnare prey."[2] Weaving a web of destruction is exactly what we do when we lie or manipulate. Deception, like any other damaging habit, takes time and determination to break. Overcoming the insatiable need to lie, control, or manipulate a situation for your best interest will be a challenge. But I am thoroughly convinced this challenge can be conquered. Will you be tempted to embellish the truth, exaggerate the facts, or even protect your reputation with a lie? Yes; but if you want to live a powerful and successful life, you must be brutally honest about your feelings, your past, and about the future you desire to create. Honesty is not only essential for physical and mental wellness but it also creates a world of opportunity.

Consider the following benefits for living a lie-free lifestyle:

- Truth is the ultimate guide to the future. "When the Spirit of truth comes, he will guide you into all the truth; for he will not speak on his own, but will speak whatever he hears, and he will declare to you the things that are to come" (John 16:13).
- Truth creates a peaceful environment. "The LORD is near to all who call on him, to all who call on him in truth" (Psalm 145:18).
- Truth builds character and self-respect. "Do your best to present yourself to God as one approved by him, a worker who has no need to be ashamed, rightly explaining the word of truth" (2 Timothy 2:15).
- Truth sanctifies. "Sanctify them in the truth; your word is truth" (John 17:17).
- Truth brings victory. "In your majesty ride on victoriously for the cause of truth and to defend the right" (Psalm 45:4).

Can you see the benefits of being honest? Take a personal challenge. Dare yourself to tell the absolute truth for the next three days. Be determined. Convey the truth in every situation, even in small things. Evaluate the outcome. I am positive you will feel refreshed and renewed and experience a new level of peace.

Are you beginning to see rejection as a friend escorting you away from deception and potentially destructive relationships? Good! Now, take a few moments to go back through this chapter, carefully highlighting the principles you have learned about falsehood and manipulation. I want to solidify these truths before we move forward in our quest to reveal the endless benefits of embracing rejection.

Chapter Principles

1. Believing a lie is as dangerous as telling one.
2. Fear is the root of untruth and will hide behind the first lie it can find.
3. Lies, untruth, and deceit are hinges that swing open the door for deception.
4. Manipulation is emotional extortion.
5. Manipulators can generate compassion from others, even when they are the ones inflicting pain.
6. Manipulators persuade victims they are the villains.
7. The number one targets for con artists and mind manipulators are those who have been emotionally wounded or rejected.
8. Fear challenges faith, and left unchecked, fear will manifest in lies and deceit.
9. Truth protects against unanticipated loss or damage.
10. Truth is our supreme liberator, greatest ally, and strongest line of defense, and it is more powerful than any bondage.

Words of Wisdom

Jesus said to him, "I am the way, and the truth, and the life. No one comes to the Father except through me."

—JOHN 14:6

Power Quote

The greatest friend of truth is time, her greatest enemy is prejudice, and her constant companion humility.

—CHUCK COLSON

Plan of Action

Perhaps you are victimized by lies you believe or imprisoned by the lies you tell. Either way, you do not have to live under the umbrella of deception. John 8:32 reveals a powerful principle: "you will know the truth, and the truth will make you free." How liberating is the truth? Let's examine this verse once again. Knowledge (learning, comprehending) of the truth (God's Word) will make (set) you free (from *any* bondage). In other words, truth produces freedom. Truth is our supreme liberator, greatest ally, and strongest line of defense, and it is more powerful than any bondage. Where is truth found? Truth is found in God's Word, the Bible. The beautiful thing is, God has written a truth-filled Book and dedicated each page to you. Discovering and applying the life-changing principles within this Book will be one of life's most rewarding accomplishments.

8

Beautiful Distortions

Watch your thoughts, for they become words.
Watch your words, for they become actions.
Watch your actions, for they become habits.
Watch your habits, for they become character.
Watch your character, for it becomes your destiny.

—AUTHOR UNKNOWN

"Can you believe Evan is only eight months old and already walking? I bet he is going to be an amazing athlete like his brother Eli.

"Did I remember to tell you, Eli scored four goals at his soccer match last night. Can you believe it? He's only six and scored all those goals?

"Kallie isn't as athletic as the boys, but her teachers just love her. In fact, her home room teacher says she is the best student she has had in years."

If you have a friend or colleague who sounds a lot

like this overindulgent mother then you understand how exhausting self-absorbed conversation can become to those on the listening end.

We all know someone who fits the description of a braggart, boaster, or smoke blower. Consider the man at work who is always showing off his new sports car or the woman at the gym boasting about her multiple vacation homes. Although they may act smug, even arrogant, egotistical conversation is a clear indication a person suffers feelings of rejection. The more people magnify their worth with self-praise, compliments, or flattery, the more apparent their insecurities become. The sad truth is, they have no idea their self-congratulatory words are working against, not for them. You are probably thinking, *Yes, I know someone who is always bragging about how much money he or she makes, dropping names of high-profile people, or showing off in childlike fashion.* Before you judge too harshly, take a step back and remember a time when you embellished the truth or showed off a little too much. Consider the outcome and perhaps repercussions of that moment. Then I will tell on myself by sharing my story.

New Shoes

I remember the first time I experienced rejection from my peers. My family relocated from Alabama to Nebraska, and I was eager to make new friends. In preparation for my first day in my new school, I received not one but two pairs of new shoes. I was certain those shoes would win the favor of two young girls I had met in our tiny trailer-park community. Excitedly, I raced home, put on my new shoes, and in a desperate attempt to impress, I walked over and casually commented on my new school shoes. One of the girls looked snidely at my shoes then at her friend and simply replied, "So?" Deflated by one word, all my self-confidence faded away. I learned a twofold lesson that day. First, true friends cannot be bought; and second, other women are hard to impress!

Life can be hard and relationships complicated. Although it is impossible to control what others say, it is possible to censor what you hear and with whom you communicate. As we journey through this chapter, I want you to become discriminating in your conversation. The reality is, over time what you hear repeated as truth will become the template for what you believe.

WORDS FRAME OUR LIVES

Words are powerful. They are so powerful that God used verbal commands to create the universe and everything in it. Have you ever wondered why God used words and not His hands or power to frame all we see? I remain captivated by the biblical account of God not only demonstrating His ability to create with words but His willingness to allow Adam to name the animals in the garden.

Let's take a closer look at allowing Adam to have the power to name the animals.

> And out of the ground the Lord God formed every [wild]
> beast and living creature of the field and every bird of the
> air and brought them to Adam to see what he would call
> them; and whatever Adam called every living creature,
> that was its name. (Genesis 2:19 AMP)

It is amazing to consider how we have power to create life and death by the words we speak. Proverbs 18:21 further emphasizes the power of our speech: "Death and life are in

It is amazing to consider how we have power to create life and death by the words we speak.

the power of the tongue, and those who love it will eat its fruits." Perhaps that is why Jesus emphasized our need to pray. He understood the connection between prayer and power. What is prayer? Prayer is conversation with your Creator. It is the verbal expression of man's desire to agree with God. When our words align with God's plans, they create access, release blessings, stop adversaries, reveal truth, and restructure our world. If what we speak has power to create, then what we say determines what we believe. Luke 6:45 highlights this truth: "The good person out of the good treasure of the heart produces good, and the evil person out of evil treasure produces evil; for it is out of the abundance of the heart that the mouth speaks."

RETURN TO SENDER

Positive people speak positive words. Destructive people speak words of destruction. Sounds rather uncomplicated, right? Not so fast. As a public speaker, I receive many let-ters, comments, and e-mails. Most of the time, the messages I receive are encouraging testimonials; however, there are exceptions. I am going to share a personal story with you because I feel you may have encountered a similar situation.

For many years, whenever I achieved a goal, whether in my personal life or within the corporate arena, I would receive a letter from a person attempting to discredit that success. The letters were carefully worded to include phrases like, *everyone thinks* or *everyone believes*. The writ-ers would use an overwhelming number of negative words and false accusations. Reading these letters profoundly impacted my emotions, making my latest achievement feel like an immense failure. For days I would battle the effects of rejection, blinded to the fact I was giving their words more power than my dreams. Today, I do not open those e-mails or letters; neither do I respond to them. They are immediately deleted or trashed upon arrival. Looking back, I see this was a wise decision. I took action and stopped fuel-ing the negative opinions of destructive people. Designed to create, words should never destroy.

The words of a stranger will never be as hurtful as words from someone you love or want to please. For instance, if a stranger calls you a "heartless, inconsiderate fool," you will likely presume that person is the "heartless, inconsid-erate fool." If, however, those words are spoken to you by your husband, mother, or friend, they become very hurtful. What you hear determines how you feel. More impor-tant, what you hear repeatedly affects what you believe.

Repetition creates validity. Harsh words, repeated often enough, become easy to believe. Remember, your eyes and ears are gateways to your mind. Make certain the words you hear are supported by God's Word and are established upon His precepts.

KALEIDOSCOPE RELATIONSHIPS

If you have peered through the lens of a kaleidoscope, you understand how beautiful distortion can look. A kaleidoscope is filled with mirrors containing colored objects such as beads or pebbles and bits of glass. As the viewer looks into one end, light entering the other creates a colorful pattern as a result of the reflection off the mirrors. Although mesmerizing at first, if you continue to look at an object through a broken lens, you will forget how things should appear and begin to view abnormal as normal. Broken and fractured, many relationships have taken on the kaleidoscope effect.

Consider my friend Sue as she describes her volatile marriage:

> I never know which husband is going to walk through the front door: Dr. Jekyll or Mr. Hyde. One day he bounds through the front door exuding with energy. The next day he walks in and doesn't mumble more than a few words the entire night. Confused by his actions, I live on pins and needles, fearful of provoking his anger. I feel as if I am riding a never-ending roller-coaster.

Sue's story is not uncommon. I could tell you countless tales of wonderful people who experience similar situations. As I mentioned earlier, the danger of remaining in a dysfunctional relationship is that it can make you forget how to function in a healthy relationship.

DESCRIPTION AND TACTICS OF THE VERBAL ABUSER

Masters at twisting words to wound and weaken their victims, verbal abusers can be hard to spot. In the next few paragraphs, I will share with you tips for identifying the shrewd and crafty villain also known as the verbal abuser. As we uncover his subtle web of words, remember, his goal is to demoralize your self-esteem. Below I have compiled a few character traits of the verbal abuser.

- Appearing friendly, outgoing, and happy-go-lucky, a closet verbal abuser may be described by others as charming, delightful, or charismatic.
- Verbal abusers reserve their most hurtful or damaging comments for times when there is no one else around to witness their behavior.
- Refusing to accept blame for their erratic behavior, verbal abusers imply their victims *push* them to act irrationally. Phrase examples include: "*You* push my buttons"; "*You* make me crazy"; "*You* are my problem."

- An experienced abuser will devalue a person's self-worth in one sentence and express sentiments of care and concern in the next.
- They covertly criticize or mock the opinions and actions of others.
- They use clever cut-downs or degrading remarks and then say, "You know I was only kidding, right?"
- They make sly suggestions. An example: "Have you thought about joining the gym? The guys at work say their wives have never looked better."
- They subtly imply failure. For instance: "Do you think you should enroll in that class? It seems a little challenging for you."
- They create competitive comparisons. Example: "Why don't you look more like your sister?"
- They imply others are incapable of making wise decisions. Example: "Is *that* what you're wearing to the party?"

Carefully wrapped and deviously packaged, verbal abuse is not always easy to detect. It is important to remember, verbal abusers tend to couch snide comments in the form of a question. That way, if their statements are challenged, they can quickly excuse away their comments. As an example, they may say, "You are misinterpreting what I said; I simply asked you a question." Their goal is to confuse their victims into believing *they* are the source of conflict.

I am no stranger to dysfunctional behavior. I have been a

bystander as a jealous groom accuses his bride of looking at the best man while still at the altar. I have witnessed a couple throw their unopened wedding gifts across the room at each other in anger. I know parents who purposefully failed to attend their son's wedding. I have watched manipulating wives withhold affection and controlling husbands withhold money. Having witnessed more than my share of dysfunction, I will in no way defend the actions of a manipulator or abuser. With that disclaimer in place, I want to take a moment and ask a few gnawing questions: What is the driving force that pushes someone to inflict verbal or physical abuse? Are some people born abusers? Is there a *cure* for jealousy, hatred, or flat-out bad behavior? Although it would take an entire book to examine these and other behavioral questions, there are a few truths I want to highlight.

Addicted to emotional chaos, abusers thrive in the atmosphere of disorder. The number one thing to remember about abusers is they maintain control of relationships by keeping their victims emotionally confused. Exhibiting erratic mood swings and being extremely pleasant one moment and erupting in a bitter tirade the next, allows verbal abusers to maintain control by keeping their victim's emotions off-balance.

Another important thing to note is abusers wallow in low self-esteem. Whether it's because they have experienced rejection or they simply feel rotten about themselves, they are compelled to tear down the self-confident. If you are in a relationship with someone who verbally abuses you, rest assured, eventually you will begin to see yourself in the same way. Trust me, no relationship is worthy of compromising your self-respect.

How do you stop abusive behavior? The reality is, abusers do not voluntarily stop the cycle of bad behavior. It is up to you. If you are in a no-win relationship, get out or get help. Remember, the goal of an abuser is to take away your individuality. Be assured they will try to alienate you from friends, family, and support groups. If you are physically threatened, call an abuse hotline or find a certified counselor. If possible, disconnect from any abusive relationship and begin forming positive associations. Mentors, influencers, and trustworthy friendships will help you get on the road to recovery.

> Spend the majority of your time with positive influences, and your life will begin to move in a positive direction.

I want to emphasize that we were not created to journey through life alone. As a matter of fact, Genesis 2:18 emphasizes this principle: "It is not good that the man should be alone." If you're going to lead a healthy, well-balanced life, you will need positive people. Spend the majority of your time with positive influences, and your life will begin to move in a positive direction.

WISDOM AND CRITICS

What is wisdom? Wisdom is advice without condemnation. What a powerful definition. One day, I asked a man whom I greatly admire to critique my work. His response caught me off guard. He said, "Tracey, I will not critique your work but I will advise you." Wow; think about the wisdom contained in that statement. Perhaps that is why King Solomon placed a high price on wisdom. In Proverbs 4:7 he writes, "Wisdom is the principal thing; therefore get wisdom: and with all thy getting get understanding" (KJV). If wisdom is to be pursued and protected, what then do we do about criticism? Are critics valuable? Is their opinion worthy of documentation? I view criticism as the highest form of verbal rejection.

One thing all successful people have in common is their share of critics. In Matthew 10:7–8, Jesus commands His disciples: "As you go, proclaim the good news, 'The kingdom of heaven has come near.' Cure the sick, raise the dead, cleanse the lepers, cast out demons. You received without payment; give without payment."

In verses 11–14 of the same chapter, He instructs,

> Whatever town or village you enter, find out who in it is worthy, and stay there until you leave. As you enter the house, greet it. If the house is worthy, let your peace come upon it; but if it is not worthy, let your peace return to you. If anyone will not welcome you or listen to your words, shake off the dust from your feet as you leave that house or town.

In essence, Jesus was saying, even when you are doing the works and will of God, you will encounter critics. He

challenged His disciples not to allow the negative opinions of unbelieving people to cling to their emotions. Jesus
talked about rejection and criticism because He understood
the depths of being misunderstood and falsely accused.
From conception to death, Jesus experienced rejection.

Rest assured Jesus understands our experiences of rejection. Jesus had His fair share of critics and came through
verbal attacks victoriously. The same power that delivered
Him from the critics of His generation will deliver you from
the naysayers of your generation. The secret to surviving
criticism is learning how to respond to judgmental words.
This process is not easy, but once mastered it will yield
great and productive rewards. Below I have listed four ways
to handle criticism.

Four Ways to Handle Criticism

1. *Pray.* With mockers and scoffers hurling accusations at Jesus, He prayed these words, "Father,
   forgive them; for they do not know what they are
   doing" (Luke 23:34). In the midst of rumors, lies,
   or false accusations, set aside time to pray. Pray for
   those who are maliciously mistreating you to repent
   and turn from the error of their ways.
2. *Analyze.* Take the opportunity to evaluate the validity of any critical comments. Stop assuming the
   voice of one equates to the voice of everyone. Critics
   use plural terminology to appear credible. Here are

a few examples of phrases critics use when they are exaggerating facts or flat-out distorting the truth: "everyone says"; "they all know"; "we believe"; "just ask anyone."

3. *Trust in God.* If you can trust God with your life, then you can also trust Him to protect your reputation.

4. *Take the high road.* Quit investing the rich commodity of time into the infertile soil of your critics. Maintain a peaceful spirit and stay focused on your future.

BITTER WORDS CAN MAKE YOU BETTER

Years ago, I traveled to the Midwest to meet with a man who had an outstanding reputation for working in the media. Excited and humbled to work with this talented man, I thought this would be one of the most defining moments of my life. Ironically, it would take many years to see how true that would be.

I will never forget the valuable lessons I learned from this man. For two grueling days, I poured out my life, heart, and passion for my calling. When our time together concluded, he stood before me and boldly spoke these words: "It has been a waste of your time and money. Your message is too hard, you're not likable, and unless you are willing to adapt, you will never make it." I returned home feeling rejected and crushed. For days I simply sat and rehearsed the bitter words. The more I rehearsed them, the more powerful they became. As I contemplated his words, I knew I had to make a decision. I could either accept his rejection as final or I could turn his rejection into a positive. I chose the latter and learned a greatest life lesson: the more you rely on God's truths, the less valuable the opinions of others become.

CONVERSATION WITH YOUR CREATOR

The greatest conversation in your life will be with your Creator. Conversation is important to God. As a matter of fact, the oldest picture we have of God and man is of them walking together, conversing in the garden. Imagine walking and conversing with God. A refreshing image, isn't it? That is exactly how God desires to interact with you. He longs for time alone to talk one-on-one with you.

> God is more interested in communicating with us than we might believe.

Prayer and meditation are two ways in which God communicates or talks with His children. God is more interested in communicating with us than we might believe. I want to share another example with you:

Now Samuel did not yet know the LORD, and the word of the LORD had not yet been revealed to him. The LORD called Samuel again, a third time. And he got up and went to Eli, and said, "Here I am, for you called me." Then Eli perceived that the LORD was calling the boy. Therefore Eli said to Samuel, "Go, lie down; and if he calls you, you shall say, 'Speak, LORD, for your servant is listening.'" So Samuel went and lay down in his place. (1 Samuel 3:7–9)

As I reflected on this passage, I realized God was more interested in speaking to a child than He was to a priest. Don't believe me? Consider that God's word bypassed a priest and went into the room to speak to a young child who was listening. By listening to and obeying the word of God, Samuel received instruction, clarification, and direction on how to approach a troubling situation. During this conversation, God revealed a powerful truth: He was going to do a new thing in the earth (1 Samuel 3:11).

Is conversation with God limited to children, priests, or a select few? No. The truth is, God is passionate about conversing with each of us. He longs to give us wisdom on how to live enjoyable and productive lives. Psalm 32:8 beautifully reveals God's heart: "I will instruct you and teach you the way you should go; I will counsel you with my eye upon you." He promises to lead us, providing step-by-step instructions on what we are to do next. His promise is to lead; our obligation is to listen. Listening for godly instruction is the first step toward receiving godly promises and rewards.

REWARD OF LISTENING

There is a verse of Scripture I have read many times. I remain amazed at how one can read a verse multiple times and yet glean a deeper meaning each time. That is what happened to me a few weeks ago as I revisited Romans 10:17, which says, "So faith comes from what is heard, and what is heard comes through the word of Christ." On the surface it seems like a simple verse. However, powerful principles are often hidden in simplistic truths. Let's take a moment and magnify these words: *faith comes by hearing.* Here is what I want to emphasize: if faith comes to us by hearing, and by faith we can have every promise of God, we should be the greatest listeners on the earth.

There is a powerful connection between the words you hear and the choices you make. Words are powerful. They create impressions, trigger memories, generate ideas, and waken emotional responses. Words can be used to energize or paralyze a person or situation. Be selective in what you hear and speak. Remember, positive words will develop a positive outlook on life and an overall positive attitude. When you have a positive attitude, you are motivated to solve problems, achieve your goals, and enjoy life.

Chapter Principles

1. When people persistently brag about their abilities or accomplishments, what they are really seeking is approval.
2. Although it is impossible to control what others say, it is possible to censor what you hear and with whom you communicate.

3. When our words align with God's plans, they create access, release blessings, stop adversaries, reveal truth, and restructure our world.

4. Like an electrical current, every relationship produces positive or negative energy. You have the choice to change the direction of the current or disengage from it altogether.

5. It is wrong to use words as weapons. Designed to create, words should never destroy.

6. Prayer is conversation with your Creator.

7. The danger of remaining in a dysfunctional relationship is that it can make you forget how to function in a healthy relationship.

8. Repetition creates validity. Harsh words often repeated become easy to believe.

9. The words of a stranger are never as hurtful as those spoken by someone you love.

10. The same power that delivered Jesus from the critics of His generation can deliver you from the naysayers of your generation.

Words of Wisdom

Let your speech always be gracious, seasoned with salt, so that you may know how you ought to answer everyone.

—COLOSSIANS 4:6

The real art of conversation is not only to say the right thing at the right place but to leave unsaid the wrong thing at the tempting moment.

—DOROTHY NEVILL

Plan of Action

The foundation of healthy relationships is effective communication. When it comes to conversation, make sure all parties are able to share their perspectives, needs, and desires. Make a concerted effort to select a place where feelings can be shared in a healthy, noncombative atmosphere. Trust and open communication will go a long way in forging long-lasting relationships.

9

Build Confidence; Laugh at Fear

Happiness is an attitude. We either make
ourselves miserable or happy and strong.
The amount of work is the same.

—FRANCESCA REIGLER

Have you ever met a homeless person who was oozing with talent and intelligence? I have. One afternoon, a charming lady named Star shared with me how her private struggles led her to inhabit the streets of skid row. I asked Star if she ever envisioned living in a homeless shelter. Her reply brought tears to my eyes. "No, Tracey, I never thought my life would turn out like this. As a child, I had big dreams and great expectations for my life. Sadly, those I loved and admired the most did not believe in my dreams."

As a child, Star was both physically and verbally abused by her parents. She describes her childhood this way:

> I felt I could never please my parents. Everything I said or did was criticized. Taught my opinions were totally valueless, I could do nothing right in their eyes. My parents would often twist and manipulate my words against me. Frequently beaten for simply answering a question, I learned, for my safety, it was best to stay silent and out of sight. I finally gave up on life and began the long journey of drugs, prostitution, and a life on the streets.

I desperately wanted to wrap my arms around Star and somehow magically reverse the events of her life, but I couldn't. Years of rejection and heartache had shattered her self-esteem. The only thing I could do was share the love of God. I taught her Jeremiah 29:11, which declares that God has a plan to prosper each of our lives. I shared Ephesians 3:20 with her, which reveals His power to accomplish abundantly far more than all we could ask or imagine. As tears poured down her sweet face, she embraced those words of truth. The wonderful part of Star's story is now, years later, she is away from the shelter and is an accomplished Bible teacher, whose goal in life is to rescue hurting women. Is it possible for people to experience similar life-changing experiences? If they are willing to embrace the heart of God that longs to say yes when others say no.

God has gifted you with enormous potential. Recognize it, build upon it, and refuse to let others strip you of it.

While your story may not be as dramatic as Star's, I feel certain you have experienced your share of disappointment, hurt, and rejection. Today, maybe you feel like no one understands the difficulties you are experiencing. God does. His desire is to heal the broken places of your life. He takes pleasure in saying yes to His children. He says, "Yes, I am your healer. Yes, I love you. Yes, I died for you. Yes, I want to prosper your life." Right now, practice saying the word *yes* aloud. Here we go. *Yes, yes, yes!* Yes feels good doesn't it? Few things conquer rejection faster than embracing God's infinite love for you. Rejection does not have to be lethal. It can actually become the ultimate guide, navigating you through the most difficult seasons in life.

REJECTION, THE ULTIMATE MOTIVATION

Most people perceive rejection as either negative or a roadblock to their future. In actuality, rejection is one of the most positive motivators on earth. Let me give you an example. Offer a small child a chocolate chip cookie as a reward for a job well done. Two things are likely to happen. They may look delighted then demand another, or you may find the cookie half-eaten between the couch cushions. Now take the same child. Let them ask for a cookie and you say no. What is the reaction this time? I imagine a full-blown emotional outburst beginning with the question, *why?*

Few people understand the positive potential the word *no* represents. *No* is a power word. Even though it is one of the smallest words in the human vocabulary, it is also one of the most influential. Unlike most negative words, *no* has a hidden honey side. In fact, *no* is as empowering as it is disabling. It reveals important information as to who's in the driver's seat of a relationship. Or equally as important, who's unwilling to assist you in fulfilling your dreams. One of the greatest attributes of the word *no* is that it makes you search for ways to achieve a yes response.

Although rejection can feel devastating, the fear of rejection is often more lethal than rejection itself. The fear of not being accepted, successful, or loved can prevent people from taking risks and bettering their futures. Fear is one of the top reasons people fail to achieve their dreams. Let's consider those who met significant rejection, yet through wisdom, faith, and positive attitudes turned the tides of success.

Thomas Edison's teachers labeled him too stupid to learn anything, yet he became a successful inventor. Edison reportedly attempted more than two thousand experiments before he developed the first incandescent lightbulb. When asked by a reporter how it felt to fail so many times, he replied, "I never failed once. I simply discovered two thousand ways it would not work."

Ted Turner was initially mocked by network executives when he unveiled his idea to create a twenty-four-hour news network. Today, his news network, CNN, is viewed in more than 212 countries around the world.

Margaret Mitchell's *Gone with the Wind* was rejected thirty-eight times before being published and winning the Pulitzer Prize in 1937. This beloved novel became one of the most popular films in cinematic history, capturing the hearts of its viewers for more than half a century.

Walt Disney International earns billions from merchandise, theme parks, and movies. However, its founder, Walt Disney, had a difficult start. A newspaper editor fired him because he said he "lacked imagination and had no good ideas." Walt Disney then started several unsuccessful businesses that ended in bankruptcy. Yet, refusing to accept failure, he eventually found a formula for success.

Warren Buffett was refused admission to Harvard University. Today he is regarded as one of the most successful investors in the world, with his net worth totaling more than forty-five billion dollars.

Albert Einstein did not speak until he was four or read until age seven. His teachers and parents perceived him as mentally handicapped and unsociable. Expelled from school and refused admittance to the Zurich Polytechnic School, against all odds, he became known as the intellectual icon of his generation and received the Nobel Prize in Physics.

Michael Jordan tried out for the varsity basketball team during his sophomore year, but at 5'11" was deemed too short to play at that level. Jordan, however, did not let this setback discourage him. With fresh motivation and discipline, he continued to develop his athletic talent and became an NBA legend. Selected as an NBA all-star fourteen times and leading his teams to six NBA championships, he earned five NBA MVP awards throughout his professional career.

R. H. Macy, founder of the immensely successful Macy's Department Store, failed seven times in business before achieving success.

Babe Ruth, famed home-run hitter and regarded by many as the greatest baseball player in history, hit 714 home runs, yet he struck out 1,330 times. His motto: "Every strike brings me closer to the next home run."[1]

Rejection is not a permission slip to quit. It is merely the fertilizer necessary to grow something powerful. In fact, successful people learn to grow their dreams in the most improbable soil and under the most severe conditions. Persistent people are powerful people. They don't give up easily or quit after the first try. They keep reaching for their goals until they do succeed.

The percentage of people who actually live out their dreams is overwhelmingly small. Why? They are afraid of what others will say if they fail. They focus on what others assume they cannot do and not what God has equipped them to do. There are two people trapped within every soul: the person they are today and the person they long to become. Your greatest challenge is not transforming the opinion of others but conquering deception of self-doubt.

Victorious people know that the secret to overcoming rejection is learning to use it as a springboard into their future. They also understand maintaining a positive attitude creates powerful energy capable of reversing past negative experiences. Money can increase your wealth, fame can magnify your favor, but only courage can extract the person you yearn to become. Ask yourself this question: when you experience rejection, do you search for a way to turn a negative comment or situation into a win? Most people neglect to consider attitude is the power key that unlocks the binding chains of rejection.

CONQUERING YOUR FEARS

What frightens you most? What image creates panic, anxiety, or worry? Take a few moments to dwell on your fear. Envision the fear coming true and then laugh. You are likely thinking, *How ludicrous. How can you expect me to laugh at my worst nightmare?* Because more than 90 percent of the things we fear most never happen. Don't believe me? When is the last time you woke up with a giant tarantula crawling up your arm? The last time a snake slithered across your feet? Or you were mercilessly stuck in an elevator for days on end? We tend to fear the improbable.

In a recent Gallup poll Americans listed things they feared the most. Number one was snakes. Any guess what number two was? That's right, public speaking. Now it is my turn to laugh.[2] Growing up, the thought of being forced to stand before a classroom of my peers and express my thoughts or opinions was horrifying. The fear so overwhelmed me, I tried to skip school if I thought I would be called upon to speak. However, the thing tormenting me most was that I did not understand why I was fearful. It took many years for me to understand I did not actually have a fear of public speaking. What I subconsciously feared was my thoughts or words would not be accepted. It took many sleepless nights to discover that I didn't fear public speaking as much as I feared rejection.

The fear of rejection is often more traumatic than real rejection. Anyone who has tried out for the varsity team, survived a lengthy court case, or applied for a job understands how the waiting process is often more stressful than the outcome. Fear of failure is paralyzing. Fear can prevent us from reaching forward with dreams, goals, or aspirations. I think it is ironic that my vocation requires me to speak to large audiences around the world. Each time I am introduced, I laugh inside. I laugh at my fear and the thought of how that fear almost prevented me from living my dream.

> The size of your fear is not nearly as important as your willingness to confront it.

What fear is keeping you from living your dream? Whose words have discouraged you or kept you from reaching for the thing or person you desire most? Fear comes in all shapes and sizes. The size of your fear is not nearly as important as your willingness to confront it. Take this opportunity to document your fears. Interrogate them. Are they based on fact? Do they act as a smokescreen keeping you from pursuing God's best for your life?

Second Timothy 1:7 declares, "God did not give us a

spirit of cowardice, but rather a spirit of power and of love and of self-discipline." Did you thoroughly read that verse? If we were to hit the rewind button and read this verse in the reverse order it would read: To have self-discipline, to possess power, and to walk in love requires you live fear free. That is powerful. Look at your list of fears, then read this verse one more time.

Which fear is keeping you from living a victorious life? Continue alternating, comparing your list of fears with this passage. Freeing, isn't it? Fears are no match for the freedom found in God's Word. Look at your list again. This time give yourself permission to laugh. When you can confidently face your greatest fear and laugh, you can master almost anything else in life.

Detoxify your Environment

Many people are afraid of flying, but that's fortunately something I never had to deal with. Believe it or not, I learned to fly an airplane at the ripe old age of nineteen. Flying amazed me because it defied logic. Even today, I still wrestle with the fact that an 875,000-pound aircraft can float effortlessly thirty thousand feet above the ground. During one of my training sessions I learned how to read an altimeter. An altimeter evaluates how much pressure is exerted in an environment, based on altitude. For instance, as altitude increases, pressure automatically decreases. Astronauts float weightlessly in outer space because there is no atmospheric resistance.

The concept I want you to glean is that the higher you go, the less pressure you should feel from outside sources. This is vital information, reminding us everything is not designed to exist everywhere. Allow me to further explain.

A few years ago, I attended a fabulous New Year's Eve party. The decorations were over-the-top, and there was enough food to feed a small army. My friends, dressed in their party best, were chattering with excitement. The topic of conversation varied from fashion favorites and vacation spots to celebrity news and local charity events. The fast-paced, ever-changing subject matter was enough to drive me to the dessert table for a slice of cake and much-needed conversational reprieve. It was there I met Lacy. Quiet and reserved, Lacy was new to our circle of friends. Eager to make her feel welcome, I invited her to join me at a small table across the room. After a few minutes of light conversation, she opened up and began to share her gripping story of courage, grief, and rejection. Lacy was like a volcano, repressed and ready for an explosive meltdown. After grasping the severity of her pain, I seriously questioned how much longer she could hold back the roaring inferno of rage. It was obvious she needed to do more than vent. She needed an emotional detoxification.

GETTING RID OF THE POISON

Two highly charged words: *emotional detoxification*. Although it may seem odd to pair these words together, they actually make a powerful team. The Free Dictionary defines *emotion* as "a state of mental agitation or disturbance."[3] Dictionary.com describes *detoxification* as a treatment designed to rid the body of poisonous substances.[4] If we combine the two definitions, it reads, *emotional detoxification*: the state of being extremely agitated, to the point of expelling unhealthy emotions from the mind, body, and spirit. Now do you see why I think these two words make the perfect tonic?

Toxic feelings are poisonous. Over time excessive, unexpressed feelings of anger, worry, fear, or unforgiveness affect mental and physical wellness. Powerfully interwoven, they are impossible to separate from your mind, body, and emotions. For instance, when you feel threatened or fearful, your blood pressure and temperature rise, your heartbeat accelerates, and your muscles tighten. Psychologists have proven it is impossible to feel strong emotion without affecting the body's physiology. Why? God linked our emotions to our physiology to regulate our actions and reactions. When one area of our life is out of balance, it affects other parts of our physiological makeup. In Lacy's case her repressed anger was creating physical infirmities and her relationships were showing signs of strain.

Release Failure and Embrace the Future

The fear of loss can create a plethora of social and relational dysfunction. I know the list would be too long of people who have remained in dead-end relationships or employment situations because they simply dread loss. Let me assure

you, if this list existed, my name would be first. I understand the conundrum of being dissatisfied with where you
are yet fearful of reaching forward. The problem with feeling discontent is it makes everyone in your environment
miserable. Without a single doubt, I promise you will be the
most miserable of all. The refusal to walk away from what
is no longer productive or enjoyable delays golden opportunities. On the flip side, by releasing broken situations,
you make way for new and positive opportunities. Think of
opportunity this way: by releasing a handful of failures, you
have open arms to embrace your future.

What does the phrase "letting go" mean? For years, I
daresay decades, I wrongly defined what it means to let
go. Rejection distorted my thinking. I was thoroughly
convinced *releasing* was synonymous with *failure.* My
perspective was entirely wrong. Stuck in wrong thinking,
I neglected to embrace the positive attributes associated
with letting go. I continued to stay in damaging relationships and bypassed fantastic career opportunities because
I misinterpreted letting go as loss. Only after many broken
relationships, unfulfilled dreams, and much prayer did my
perspective on letting go change. When I became aware
of the many benefits associated with change, the light
switch in my mind turned on. For the first time, I caught
a glimpse of the truths rejection had tried to keep hidden. One principal truth being, you cannot reach for your
future if your hands are bound tightly to your past. If you
are holding on to something damaging or unproductive,

today is the perfect time to let go. Below are positive reasons to flush the past and move forward.

Discover Healthy Relationships

"There is no fear in love, but perfect love casts out fear; for fear has to do with punishment, and whoever fears has not reached perfection in love."

— 1 JOHN 4:18

Although tempting, revisiting the past will not change how a relationship ends. Yes, given a specific scenario, your choices or responses may be different, but typically the outcome remains the same. Wrong relationships do not work. Dwelling on the past creates suffering, leaving you emotionally enslaved to the past. Climbing through the trash can of yesterday just gets you dirty. Make better use of your time by focusing on the lessons you have learned, and apply those nuggets of truth to future relationships. Above all, prepare your heart to receive love.

Exchange Pain for Joy

"Very truly, I tell you, you will weep and mourn, but the world will rejoice; you will have pain, but your pain will turn into joy."

— JOHN 16:20

When asked about his divorce, John explains it this way:

I married Juliana, my high school sweetheart and the most beautiful woman I've ever known. Our marriage was like a fairy tale come true. She was my best friend and confidant, and I will never love another woman with the passion I loved her. I can't believe it has been twenty years since she left me.

Tell me, what emotional glitch makes a person cling to the past when the future is right before his eyes? Although John claims he is ready for a new relationship, he's probably not. Nothing screams, "I'm not ready" like repeated trips down memory lane. Notorious for first-date blunders, John's incessant ramblings about his ex-wife and their dysfunctional marriage sent women scrambling for the door. If you are clinging to your past, would-be candidates for your future will likely run in the opposite direction. Let's stop for a moment and consider the truth.

When it comes to relationships, it's as if many of us have stood at the bus stop, ticket in hand, yet fail to board because we are too mesmerized by the bright red taillights of the bus we just missed. It is time to stop romanticizing memories of days gone by and start focusing on potential relationships. Maybe if we all dropped to our knees and counted our blessings, we would recognize the potential that lies in front of us. For some, that includes the blessing of being single. If you are not currently involved with a romantic interest, enjoy the luxury of devoting yourself to your passion or forming new and exciting relationships. Focus on the positive, and you will feel less like a victim.

Experience Freedom from Past Wounds

"He heals the brokenhearted,
and binds up their wounds."

—Psalm 147:3

During the medieval period of European history, violence prevailed. Cruel acts of ruthless brutality were carried out upon criminals, conspirators, and unfortunately sometimes the innocent. One torture device, a contraption designed to stretch its victims in opposing directions, inflicted great mental suffering and physical pain. It's a device I am sure I do not want to experience firsthand. But consider what happens when you try to hold the past with one hand and reach for the future with the other. Stretched in separate directions you remain trapped, suspended between the drama of yesterday and the dream of tomorrow. Holding onto two worlds is torturous. No one is designed to live in the past and future simultaneously. It is time to unlock the cuffs shackling you to the torture chamber of your past. Release regrets. Slam shut the door of shame and then walk through the door of endless opportunity.

Develop and Grow

"Beloved, I do not consider that I have made it
my own; but this one thing I do: forgetting what
lies behind and straining forward to what lies
ahead, I press on toward the goal for the prize
of the heavenly call of God in Christ Jesus."

—Philippians 3:13-14

The most common complaint I hear from disgruntled couples is, "It's just not fair; my spouse is not acting like the person I fell in love with." Generally, that is true. My response, however, is, "Neither are you." It is entirely unfair to imagine the fun, extroverted, gushing person you marry at twenty will be the serious, mature, sophisticated spouse you have at forty. Common sense says you shouldn't expect them to be. Change is vital to growth. When my daughter was young, she despised change. The thought of things changing terrified her because she interpreted change as loss. It took time to persuade her to view change as a necessary bridge linking today with the future. If you genuinely care for someone, give them space and opportunity to grow. Remember, the only people who do not change are those who stop living.

There are people and opportunities that do not qualify for your future. Dreams change, people change, children grow up, friends grow apart, and opportunity will come and go faster than we can blink. Like the winds that go ahead of a nor'easter, storm clouds are a sure sign change is on the horizon. In the same way, rejection is one of the greatest indicators that it is time to embrace change as a new and welcome friend.

Chapter Principles

1. Few things conquer rejection faster than embracing God's infinite love for you.

2. Rejection does not have to be lethal. It can actually become the ultimate guide, navigating you through the most difficult seasons in life.

3. Attitude is the power key that unlocks the binding chains of rejection.

4. Maintaining a positive attitude creates energy.

5. The fear of failure is paralyzing. It can prevent a person from fulfilling his or her dreams, goals, or aspirations.

6. Emotional detoxification is the state of being extremely agitated, to the point of expelling unhealthy emotions from the mind, body, and spirit.

7. It is impossible to feel strong emotions without affecting the body's physiology.

8. You cannot reach for your future if your hands are bound tightly to your past.

9. No one is designed to live in the past and future simultaneously.

10. Rejection is one of the greatest indicators that it is time to embrace change as a new and welcome friend.

Words of Wisdom

The LORD is my light and my salvation; whom shall I fear? The LORD is the stronghold of my life; of whom shall I be afraid?

—PSALM 27:1

Power Quote

If you don't like something, change it; if you can't change it, change the way you think about it.

—MARY ENGELBREIT

Plan of Action

Each day presents the opportunity to gain a positive and optimistic attitude. I assure you, life will not always go as planned, and many times you will be the only person in your cheering section. The secret is learning to become self-motivated during difficult seasons of change. The greatest motivator I have discovered is the Bible. I encourage you to memorize, write, confess, and live its life-changing principles and watch fear fall by the wayside. God is not the originator of fear but the author of peace.

10

The New You

*Be beautiful if you can, wise if you want
to, but be respected—that is essential.*

—ANNA GOULD

As I was flipping through a magazine one day, my eyes fell on an advertisement featuring a kitten gazing into a full-length mirror. What grabbed my attention was that the image reflected in the mirror was not of a kitten but a ferocious lion. This tiny kitten perceived himself king of the jungle. With all confidence I believe his *meow* sounded to him like a *roar*.

When you look into the mirror, what do you see? Do you envision a confident career woman, loving father, or community leader? Or is your reflection a snapshot of a brokenhearted child trying to mask the pain of rejection? Only you know the truth. My goal is to help you identify the *real you*. I'm not referring to personality, image, or corporate identity, but rather the person you long to become.

While I cannot guarantee you a perfect life, understanding and applying the following principles will empower you to have a successful and joyous life.

I want to begin by talking about your future. More specifically, I want to help you identify your dreams and the role rejection plays in fulfilling those dreams. Throughout this chapter, I am going to reveal practical ways to use rejection as a catalyst to launch you into your future.

Dreamers

I love being around dreamers. As a matter of fact, my closest friends and mentors are dreamers. Enthusiastic, positive, and self-assured, they are not easily lured by the entrapment of insecurity. Having faced the perilous pit of rejection on more than one occasion, they understand the importance of remaining anchored to their dreams.

When I think about dreamers, Cynthia immediately comes to mind. As a stay-at-home mom, Cynthia was away from the job market for more than twenty years. When her children were grown and away at college, she accepted a receptionist position at a local real estate firm. Quick-witted and a sharp thinker, Cynthia was quickly promoted and encouraged by her office manager to join their sales team. After months of online real estate classes, she took the Realtor's examination for licensing and failed. She took the test a second time and failed yet again. A third attempt yielded the same unsuccessful result. The magnificent part of Cynthia's story is she refused to accept failure as defeat. Rather than walking away from her dreams, in order to escape rejection, she worked toward them with greater fervency and expectation of success. Succeed she did. Today she is the owner of a real estate corporation, and her brokerage firm is one of the top-grossing businesses in the northeast.

Sadly, not all of my friends have survived the slippery slopes of rejection with such ease. As you read the stories below, I want you to think about your dreams and consider how rejection plays an influential role in achieving them.

One dear lady shared with me,

Last fall, I traveled with two friends on a business trip to Los Angeles. Having worked in the fashion industry for years, I was toying with the idea of starting a boutique-style clothing line of my own. Hoping for words of encouragement, I shared my business proposal with my friends. The words I received were a far cry from encouraging; in fact, they belittled my plans and discounted my ideas. In a moment my creative energy dissipated as a wave of fear washed over my heart. I went home, shelved my plans, and buried my dream. One year later a business associate within my company launched a similar clothing line and it was a huge success. The greatest mistake I made was listening to the discouraging words of my friends.

Friends are not the only ones who dismiss our dreams. Consider Vince's story.

My childhood dream was to become an engineer. The thought of developing office suites, high-rise condominiums, and buildings kept me awake at night. I envisioned owning a successful construction company and growing it into a global business. Although I had significant dreams, my father had an entirely different set of blueprints for my life. He persuaded me to carry on the family business, a local car dealership established by my grandfather. I forsook my dream of becoming an engineer only to fail miserably in the automobile industry. Each time I travel to the city I live with the regret of not pursuing my dream.

Guess what? The percentage of people who actually live out their dreams is overwhelmingly small. Why? Most people live in fear of what people will say if they fail. Don't think for one moment we haven't all slammed the brakes on our dreams because of something someone said. I'll be the first to confess, there were times when words from a negative person cut so deep I packed up my dreams and recoiled into seclusion. We have all made this mistake. I know how irresistible the temptation is to connect, fit in, and relate. In reality, fearing the opinions of others destroys our dreams at a faster rate than outright failure. Our human dilemma is no one wants to feel like the freak who is always failing, but neither do we want to blend into anonymity. The truth is, there are two types of people within each of us: the chameleon content to camouflage his way through life and the dreamer who detests conformity. For many, the dreamer within has been asleep far too long. It's time for you wave good-bye to the naysayers, skeptics, and critics; dust away the cobwebs collecting on your dreams; and begin living a life filled with purpose.

SNAPSHOTS OF THE FUTURE

Dreams are like picture windows allowing us to see our potential through the eyes of God. Like snapshots of the future, dreams disclose divine prospects and promises. The ability to dream is a divine trait. I am convinced we are never more like our Creator than when we are mapping out our dreams. Perhaps that is why I remain completely baffled by people who are without dreams. Please do not misunderstand. I would never pass judgment on someone who chooses not to dream. What I have discovered is nondreamers are often first in line to undermine the plans of those who do dream.

> Dreams are like picture windows allowing us to see our potential through the eyes of God.

Let's examine the life of Joseph, the Bible's greatest dreamer. If his worth had been based on the opinions cast forth by his family, we would label him a big fat zero. In contrast to their opinions he was anything but average and far from being a loser. Intelligent, sensitive, and courageous, Joseph was blessed. The problem for Joseph was he was stuck in his hometown of Canaan. Location matters. It turned out he had a powerful gift of interpreting dreams, but in Canaan, no one knew. You may possess a powerful gift, but in the wrong place, your gift is quickly devalued. For example, the thought of owning a new luxury car sounds exciting to most people. But to a man trapped on a desert island, where there are no roads to drive on, gasoline for fuel, people to visit, or places to go, the luxury car is quickly devalued. In the same way, the gift within you will only be magnified when you discover the place and the people to whom you have been assigned.

On several occasions, Joseph faced the bitter blows of rejection. Cast into a pit by his brothers, sold as a slave, falsely accused, and wrongly imprisoned, his ability to interpret dreams may have died with him. The remarkable truth is that each act of rejection led him to the king's palace. In Egypt, from the jail to the palace, people were dreaming and Joseph's gift for interpreting dreams prospered. Proverbs 18:16 reveals the power of following our dreams: "A gift opens doors; it gives access to the great." What assurance, to know in the face of being discarded, misunderstood, or abandoned—our dreams bring us great reward.

THE PERFECT LIFE

Have you ever dreamed of having the perfect life? What personal achievements come to mind? Are you winning an award, building a corporation, or retiring with great wealth? When you think about those images, what emotions do you feel? Are you happy? Do you feel accepted and confident? Now let's compare the ideal life with real life. What feelings flood your mind when you contrast your dream life with the life you are living? Are you excited or overwhelmed? Does dreaming evoke energy or depression?

Before we jump into the deep end of the discussion, let's talk about some of the benefits of dreaming. While the benefits of dreaming are far too many to list, below I have highlighted a few of my favorites. Please take time to add to this list and journal about the rewards of pursuing your dreams.

- Dreams clarify your inner thoughts, aspirations, and desires.
- Writing about your dreams is simply organizing and documenting what is most important to you.
- Dreaming exposes opportunities overlooked by others.
- Dreaming helps you distinguish what is not important to you.
- Dreams reveal distractions and counterfeit opportunities.
- Dreaming forces you to create an achievable plan of action.

With so many magnificent reasons to dream, why do some resist reaching for their dreams? Too many people neglect to embrace their dreams because they are terrified of how people will respond. The sad thing is, they secretly long to fulfill their dreams, but years of rejection, discouraging words, or past failures prevent them from pursuing their hearts' desires. The comparison of the life they long to experience and the life they are living often evokes feelings of inadequacy, self-rejection, and defeat. Psychologically they are convinced, "Nothing good ever happens to me, so why should I set myself up for failure?" As a result they become content to live dreamless lives. Personally, I find a dreamless life totally unacceptable.

If dreaming is so important, how do we avoid the pitfalls designed to sandbag our potential? I can assure you it takes a perceptive person not to fall prey to the bleating cry of failure.

Conquering the deception of self-doubt is one of the greatest challenges in life. Think about the word *self-doubt*. Now say it aloud. Doesn't it sound disabling? It is. Like a shredder that latches on to a piece of paper, self-doubt slashes our self-confidence into a million tiny pieces. Doubt detours our dreams, exposes feelings of inadequacy, and erodes confidence. Self-doubt is the voice inside your mind that makes your life seem insignificant when compared to your dreams. It continually whispers in your ear, "You're not good enough"; "You will never succeed"; "Stop trying"; or "Others think you are crazy." Don't be fooled. Doubt is the doorkeeper of dysfunction.

GOLD MEDALS

Although I take no pleasure in this confession, I must admit it's true. If gold medals were given for dysfunctional behavior, women would win hands down. Yes, I said it. For the life of me I cannot name a single woman who hasn't treated doubt and fear as familiar friends. Most of the time fear assumes top spot as best friend. The fascinating thing about fear is that it has an outfit for every season and situation. Send fear an invitation to your next pity party. I guarantee it has a masquerade costume customized for the occasion. That is what fear does best. It masquerades as truth. It derails us from moving forward with our dreams and reroutes us away from our purpose. How then do we move beyond the ill-effects of self-doubt? How do we master feelings of incompetence or failure? If we are sincere about changing, we must stop doing things that destroy our identities.

Push the pause button. I want to clarify the terms *confidence* and *identity*. Confidence is placing assurance in something or someone. Identity is assurance of ownership. Individuals who refer to themselves as *children of God* are simply recognizing their distinction as *heir* or *successor* to His kingdom. It is a term used to acknowledge their identities. Surprisingly, many of the same people who identify with being part of God's heavenly kingdom lack confidence in fulfilling their earthly goals or dreams.

Unlike identity, confidence can prove very unpredictable. Up one day, down the next. Strong on Sunday, it is eating dust by Tuesday. I have watched confidence come and go in a matter of milliseconds. I have looked on as top athletes slide down this slippery slope on more than one occasion. Losing a few games in a row, their confidence declines, and they free-fall into a season-long performance slump. The same thing happens when a top salesman loses a handful of clients, a model gains a few pounds, a band loses a few gigs, professional speakers lose their train of thought, or writers drop off the bestseller list. The truth is no one performs perfectly all the time. Believing otherwise will leave you victim to the devouring wolves of rejection. Managing your personal confidence level is essential. Below are a few ways to help build and balance your personal confidence.

Know Your Worth

I feel as if I will come unraveled if I hear one more person say they have nothing to offer the world. Somewhere, someone needs your knowledge or expertise. You have the answer to someone's personal crisis. If you can cook, change a diaper, shovel snow, fix a flat tire, or read a book, you have knowledge others need. Your life is valuable, but only you can define your worth.

It only takes a visit to a department store dressing room to grasp how critical and insecure women truly are. As my daughter and I were shopping last week, we overheard these phrases: "This dress makes my chest look small"; "These jeans make my hips look wide"; "I need taller high heels; I'm way too short"; "Can you see if they have any flats; I feel like a giant"; "I'm too skinny; I don't have any curves"; "I'm too fat and have too many curves." Trust me, men, I could go on with the list of comments all day. Insecurity is the real reason women like to go shopping with a girlfriend.

We know firsthand the negative thoughts that bombard our minds and the comments needed to diffuse them. What is important is learning how to decrease negative self-talk. We do ourselves a world of injustice by emphasizing our weaknesses. If you want your husband to forget about your big hips, quit talking about them. Gluttons for punishment, we take out giant yellow highlighters and draw attention to the very things we want others to overlook. Stop underscoring negative attributes you want others to forget.

DEMAND RESPECT

For more than a year, Angela has been a whipping post for her boyfriend's verbal abuse, which includes calling her nasty names and belittling her dreams. Angela's self-esteem is a fraction of what it was before their relationship. Frightened and alone, she believes her boyfriend's lies and clamors for his approval.

A single mother of three neglects to correct her sixteen-year-old son for fear he will physically abuse her.

Ryan, a sixth grader, is bullied by older boys who threaten physical harm if he doesn't pay them off every Friday. Who would believe it, children extorting other children?

Bullying isn't limited to young people. Sandra, a single mom, faces grueling sexual harassment at work. Ignoring the sly innuendoes and overt gestures, she overlooks the sleazy comments to keep her job.

Shawn lost ten thousand dollars in commissions to a

colleague who ripped off his account. New to the corporation and not wanting to make enemies, he disregarded the power play.

The fear of rejection is costly. Truthfully, the price tag of rejection is more than most of us can afford. We can hide in fear and pretend slanderous words don't hurt, but they do. We can run from bullies on the playground, and odds are we will still be running from them in the workplace.

I have had my share of confidence crushers. I know what it is like to be a doormat for the emotionally disturbed and chronic verbal abuser. Regretfully, I am sure you have encountered similar if not equally disturbing experiences. How then do we stop the claws of rejection from tearing into our backsides? What is the solution? Is there a solution? Two things are guaranteed to turn the tide on rejection. One is confidence; the other respect. Trust me, the direct correlation between the self-esteem you model and the level of honor and respect others express toward you is enormous.

When you show a high regard for yourself, ideas, or beliefs, others will follow your example. In fact, studies reveal confident, outgoing, self-assured people are less likely to engage or stay in abusive relationships. It is time we walk in confidence and reclaim our self-esteem.

In Aretha Franklin's super-hit "Respect," she vividly describes her need and demand for "a little respect." Respect should be a nonnegotiable, mutual exchange in every relationship. If you are not receiving the respect you deserve, ask for it. If asking doesn't work, demand it. Explain to others how their negative comments or other injurious actions make you feel. Then set up and enforce behavior guidelines. If the terms of your relationship are not honored, drop the relationship.

BE AWARE OF YOUR PERSONAL PRESENTATION

How many times have I heard the complaint, "They don't know me, and already they don't like me"? Whether or not this is a valid complaint, let's take a moment and consider the self-portrait you are presenting. Body language is the preamble of your personal presentation. It conveys who you *think* you are. Your demeanor speaks volumes. Observe a woman as she walks into a room. Does she seemingly float into the room, or does she exhibit a persona that says, *This is the last place on earth I want to be*? Are her shoulders slumped? Is she sloppily dressed? Do her eyes stay glued to the floor? If so, she is creating a visual image of someone who feels unworthy and insecure. This time I want you to imagine a woman entering the room with her head held high, shoulders back, and eager to engage in conversation. She successfully creates an impression of confidence, and others are drawn to her. Notice the difference? Remember, your appearance is the nonverbal, outward representation of how you feel about yourself.

PLEASE TELL ME NO

Will I always struggle with insecurity? The answer depends on your attitude toward people or things that leave you feeling vulnerable. The problem with rejection is, it makes us horribly insecure. Insecurity robs us of our confidence, and a lack of confidence makes us discard the greatest card in the deck—the dream card. A university survey reported, on average, a one-year-old child hears the word *no* more than four hundred times a day. Another study estimates a child will hear the words *no* or *don't* more than 148,000 times while growing up, compared to only a few thousand *yes* messages. At first I thought this must be an exaggerated statistic, but consider that one of the first words we learn to speak is *no*. The harsh truth is we are programmed to expect *no* in answer to our questions, desires, and dreams. A constant diet of *no* creates feelings of shame, self-doubt, and rejection.

Think about the last time someone told you *no*. How did you respond? Did you fight to reverse the *no* response or simply accept *no* as the final verdict? Take time to relive a moment when someone answered your problem or dream with a *yes*. How did you feel? The word *yes* sounds good, doesn't it? While life may throw a dozen or more *no*s at you every day, there are hundreds of ways you can maintain a *yes* attitude. What dream would you pursue if negative words, like *no* or *failure*, were not part of the dream equation? Now imagine the dream you would pursue if you could dispel your hidden fears. To encourage your dreams, I have written out my favorite Scripture verses that highlight the importance of purpose.

- "The human mind may devise many plans, but it is the purpose of the LORD that will be established." (Proverbs 19:21)
- "But this is why I have let you live: to show you my power, and to make my name resound through all the earth." (Exodus 9:16)
- "I cry to God Most High, to God who fulfils his purpose for me." (Psalm 57:2)

Perhaps rejection has wrecked your plans and left your dreams dangling on life support. I wonder how many are honest enough to admit that their dreams are struggling to survive. When marriages crumble, children run away, friends turn their backs, and careers fade, purpose remains.

I want to close this chapter by sharing a powerful passage penned by Marianne Williamson:

Our deepest fear is not that we are inadequate. Our deepest fear is that we are powerful beyond measure. It is our light, not our darkness, that most frightens us. We ask ourselves, who am I to be brilliant, gorgeous, talented, fabulous? Actually, who are you not to be? You are a child of God. Your playing small doesn't serve the world. There's nothing enlightened about shrinking so that other people won't feel insecure around you. We are all meant to shine, as children do. We were born to make manifest the glory of God that is within us. It's not just in some of us; it's in everyone. And as we let our own light shine, we unconsciously give other people permission to do the same. As we're liberated from our own fear, our presence automatically liberates others.[1]

Chapter Principles

1. Most people live in fear of what other people will say if they fail.

2. Fearing the opinions of others destroys dreams at a faster rate than flat-out failure.

3. The human dilemma is that no one wants to feel like someone who always fails, but neither does anyone want to blend into anonymity.

4. Dreams are like picture windows that allow us to see our potential through the eyes of God.

5. Like snapshots of the future, dreams disclose divine prospects and promise.

6. Nondreamers are often first in line to undermine the plans of those who do dream.

7. Writing your dreams is simply organizing and documenting what is most important.

8. Doubt detours our dreams, exposes feelings of inadequacy, and erodes confidence.

9. Fear masquerades as truth.

10. The price tag of rejection is more than most can afford.

Words of Wisdom

Jesus looked at them and said, "For mortals it is impossible, but not for God; for God all things are possible."

—MARK 10:27

Power Quote

To accomplish great things, we must not only act, but also dream; not only plan, but also believe.

—ANATOLE FRANCE

Plan of Action

Someone once said, "The only difference between a rut and a grave is how deep it is and how long you're in it." I agree. Falling into a rut is not always avoidable. Staying long enough to dig your own grave is quite another story. Today, if you feel as if life is burying you alive, the first thing you must do is stop digging and start planting.

Life will never change until you decide to think and move in a positive direction. The road to emotional healing can be challenging. If you spend your time replaying past events, you will have little energy to prepare for the things in your future. It is time to stop digging in the past. The only thing you are likely to find there is more dirt.

11

Wave Good-bye
to Your Past

If you don't design your own life plan, chances
are you'll fall into someone else's plan. And guess
what they have planned for you? Not much.

—TONY ROBBINS

Imagine you have the ability to create your own world—a perfect utopia designed by you. What environment would you create? Who would you invite to live there? How would you spend your time? Would you invent, design, or simply enjoy the pleasures of the atmosphere you created? Go ahead, take some time, contemplate the idea, let your mind wander, and allow your creativity to flow. Is your world perfect yet? Are you at total peace? Is there anything you would change? Rather exhausting, isn't it?

Creating our own world is an overwhelming concept.

Yet in reality we attempt to do this every day. We make decisions based on immediacy, emotion, and limited perspective. Is it any surprise we wake up one day and question, "Who created this mess anyway?" Perhaps the reason for our frustration, depression, or outright dissatisfaction with life is that we, created beings, are attempting a task only our Creator is capable of accomplishing. Interestingly, the first words of the Bible are, "In the beginning . . . God." He clarified His existence before He created anything or anyone. Likewise, we must clearly define who we are before we road map our future. Success and fulfillment begin with a plan of action. Peace, joy, and contentment cannot coexist with chaos. The foundation to living a victorious life is to have a God-centered identity—an identity man cannot steal and circumstances cannot seize.

WHO AM I?

As a mentor and consultant, the first question I usually ask a client is, "How would you describe yourself?" Most respond with a formal title like president, CEO, or founder. Others will emphasize their accomplishments, such as, "former NFL player" or "five-star chef." Still others use relational responses, like "I'm John's mother" or "Jeff's wife." Few people separate who they are from what they do or who they know. If you are going to defeat the negative attributes of rejection, you must discover who you are and for what purpose you were created. It is time to step out of the muck and mire, to rip the rug right out from under rejection and boldly pursue your future.

Your life has purpose and meaning. Are you ready to discover it? Are you willing to look past the failures of yesterday and try again? Will you resist the urge to assess your life based on the opinion of others? Your life is significant. Perhaps hidden within you is the answer to a great medical mystery, the compassionate heart of a humanitarian, or the insightful wisdom of a mother who will help develop the next generation of leaders and entrepreneurs. You will never know until you make an honest life assessment. When you discover who you are, you will begin fulfilling the purpose for which you were created.

Virtual Worlds

Amused and somewhat amazed, I discovered there are many websites designed to help you create a personalized virtual world. On the surface, it looks very appealing as the opportunities are endless. In a virtual word you can start afresh, design the life you always desired, and become the successful person you knew you could become. It is a place where mansions are built in a day, butlers butter your bagels, and no-limit charge cards belong to you. There are no tan lines, worries, or wrinkles. Youth is eternal, money always accessible, and there is no extravagance you cannot afford. You have perfect friends, a perfect spouse, perfect children, and you are a perfect person. Does this sound unrealistic, over-the-top, or superficial? It is. The harsh reality is, virtual worlds are not the worlds in which we live. There are no perfect people, professions, or societies.

ISLAND MENTALITY

To help us capture a clear snapshot of your personal image, let's begin with a multiple-choice challenge. This simple quiz will assist you in understanding *how* you view yourself and your past, and will unveil any dream destroyers. This scenario is purposefully exaggerated to help better reflect your true self-identity.

After saving all year, imagine rewarding yourself with a cruise to the South Pacific. The first few days of the cruise are smooth sailing. But on the third day, hurricane winds blow, the ship is destroyed, and you find yourself alone on a desolate island. Months pass with no sign of human activity. Suddenly, a tiny canoe appears with two neighboring island natives. When asked who you are, you begin to: (please choose A, B, or C)

A. Retell your life story. Explaining this is just one more tragic event in a long list of injustices, you express that you're not really surprised this happened and scold yourself for expecting a rewarding vacation. Turning to the natives, you make it clear you don't expect them to understand your dilemma but thank them for taking time to listen. When they

invite you to a neighboring island for dinner, you
woefully decline.

B. Brag on your accomplishments. In vivid detail, you
describe the awful events you encountered, carefully highlighting the survival skills you employed
to stay alive. When invited to a neighboring island
for dinner, you thank them but decline explaining
you have six months of meals already prepared.

C. Cynically ramble off a list of personal philosophies.
You argue the storm was not a result of providen-
tial intervention but rather a simple matter of cause
and effect. When invited to a neighboring island for
dinner, you say, "I would love to attend, but I'm sure
fate has other plans."

Assessment of Answers

If your answer was "A," then your dream destroyer is a
negative self-image.

Isn't it funny how it takes most of us nine months to
choose the perfect name for a baby and then we question if
we made the right choice? I wonder what Isaac and Rebecca
were thinking when they chose the name Jacob, meaning
"deceiver, cheater, or defrauder." I imagine each time Jacob
heard his name called, he instinctively cringed. Liar . . .
cheater . . . con artist. He had to question, "Will I become
more than what my name suggests?" I believe the more he
contemplated the negative words ascribed to his character,
the more he subconsciously believed them. As so many do,

he eventually became the thing he listened to and feared most. Let's take a moment and examine a life-altering encounter from his colorful past:

> Jacob was left alone; and a man wrestled with him until daybreak. When the man saw that he did not prevail against Jacob, he struck him on the hip socket; and Jacob's hip was put out of joint as he wrestled with him. Then he said, "Let me go, for the day is breaking." But Jacob said, "I will not let you go, unless you bless me." So he said to him, "What is your name?" And he said, "Jacob." Then the man said, "You shall no longer be called Jacob, but Israel, for you have striven with God and with humans, and have prevailed." (Genesis 32:24–28)

Interestingly, God used a broken hip to heal a broken heart. Crisis brought Jacob to the place where he was more concerned with God's opinion than with man-made labels. It took wrestling, waiting, and work, but the result was worth the prize. Although family and friends incorrectly branded Jacob, God knew there was a prince buried beneath the tough exterior of a wounded heart. Is there a prince or princess hidden on the inside of you? God knows, and I suspect beneath heartache and pain, you know. Have there been times when others have spoken failure over your life? If so, I want you to create an inventory of all the amazing things that lie hidden within you. Divide your page into columns and then in vivid detail describe your positive attributes. Include your physical, mental, social, and creative characteristics. Recall past personal successes and traits or attitudes that made you successful. Be sure to highlight a positive word you would use to describe yourself. Finally, list ways God can use you to heal the hurts of others.

If your answer was "B," then your dream destroyer is self-reliance.

I want to let you in on a little secret. The reason some people seem overly self-confident or self-sufficient is they are very insecure. Somewhere in their private journeys they were made to feel incompetent or hopeless. Insecurity is often a result of insufficient provision, education, or emotional stability during childhood. The truth is, those who strive to keep up an appearance of being prepared, competent, and beyond needing the help of others are desperately screaming for approval and positive verbal affirmation. Healing from insecurity begins the moment we acknowledge our insufficiencies and allow God to mend our broken places.

The success of your dreams will require the involvement of others. Encouragement and investment in your dream will often come from the unlikeliest of sources. I have many dynamic stories of people who volunteered their time, spoke an encouraging word, or through financial support proved an essential part of my life story. People enter our lives for various reasons. Some are connectors, motivators, guardians, comforters, or advisers. It is important we do not miss an opportunity for a divine connection. There is someone who holds an important key to your future. Discover, recognize, and reward them.

If your answer was "C," then your dream destroyer is doubt.

Have you heard the proverb, "If it is too good to be true, then it probably is"? Although this is somewhat true, it is not always the case. Will you take a moment to complete this quiz to determine if you're a cynic?

Circle the number(s) of those you agree with:
1. I refuse to watch the news or read the paper because they are filled with lies.
2. Self-help programs, seminars, and books are for mindless failures who are potential cult followers.
3. Counseling is for the weak-minded who live in the drama of yesterday.
4. Class reunions are for the "Now I am better than you" crowd.
5. I don't know why I am reading this book—how can a book change anything?

Surely, you just laughed. After all, who would be so cynical? Remember the TV show *All in the Family*? Archie Bunker, the main character, made a generation laugh at his outlandish ethnic and gender profiling. Why did we laugh? Because we thought, *Surely no one could be this negative and cynical.* Wrong. The sad truth is, while we were laughing, he never did. Cynics rarely laugh. You may see an occasional smirk break through, but rarely a smile. Yes, many things in life cannot be changed. A leopard cannot change its spots, but you can change *you.* Your outlook and perspective can change, beginning today.

Do-Overs

Do you remember running through the sprinkler on a hot summer day? Playing ball on a vacant lot? If your childhood was anything like mine, you remember the endless teasing, bike riding, and the dares of friends mischievously challenging you to perform some brave act. And if a dare were exceptionally dangerous, they used the words of ultimate persuasion: "I double-dare you." Double-dares were thrilling. They separated the talkers from the risk-takers. Succeeding at a double-dare meant gaining the affirmation and cheers of your friends. If, however, you failed, the only way to save face was protesting an injustice, claiming the dare was unreasonable or someone misrepresented the challenge. A true competitor learned to make a persuasive argument and then cry, "No fair! I deserve a do-over." That was a ten-year-old's way of saying, "I messed up, and I need another try to succeed."

Have you ever wished you could have a do-over in life?

Are you disappointed with the direction your life has taken or longingly wish you could hit a reset button on life and begin again? If so, you should start celebrating! The good news is you can start life anew. Second Corinthians 5:17 explains it best: "If anyone is in Christ, there is a new creation: everything old has passed away; see, everything has become new!"

ESCAPE OR RECOVER

Visualize working on your laptop. Everything is running smoothly, your work is nearing completion, and then suddenly a warning sign flashes across the screen: "System failure!" Immediately you face two choices: select the escape button to delete files or choose recovery mode to save files. At this moment you must select wisely, because the choice you make will determine what information will be saved or deleted. Selecting the escape option will erase all previous content, providing you with a fresh, clean page upon which to write. If, however, you choose the recovery mode option, the computer will search the existing hard drive in an effort to retrieve and restore all information previously entered. In essence, you are not creating new information but simply restoring old or outdated information. Life is unpredictable. Seasons change. People change. One day your life is running smoothly, the next unexpected problems arise and you are thrown into the system failure cycle of life. In the blink of an eye you have two options: escape or recover. Both are acceptable.

There are many reasons to start life over, such as crisis

Get excited about your future. Look forward to new experiences, and believe your dreams can come true.

and opportunity. Crisis may force you to start life over, but opportunity gives you a license to start over. Stop waiting for a crisis to send you an invitation to pursue your heart's desire. Instead, get excited about your future. Look forward to new experiences, and believe your dreams can come true.

PREDICTING THE FUTURE

The greatest predictor of your future is how long it takes you to let go of your past. In Scripture we are commanded to look forward, not backward. The story of Lot's wife highlights the importance of letting past experiences go while reaching forward to the future. God gave Lot and his family the opportunity to escape the city of Sodom. He clearly warned them not to stop or look back. Tragically, Lot's wife did not follow the command, and destruction overtook her (Genesis 19:26).

In what area of your life have you been delivered? Have you been rescued from a destructive relationship or a treacherous experience? Remember to listen to God's instruction and stop trying to walk through doors He has closed. The thought of beginning life again can seem overwhelming. But take a few moments and imagine what life will be like if you are unwilling to embrace change.

1. Until you have revelation of the treasure hidden within you, others will never behold it.

2. Success and fulfillment begin with a plan of action.

3. The foundation to living a victorious life is having a God-centered identity, an identity man cannot steal and circumstances cannot seize.

4. Often brokenness is a prerequisite to healing.

5. Crisis may *force* you to start life over, but opportunity gives you a *license* to start over.

6. The people belonging in your future are excitedly awaiting your arrival.

7. When you begin to discover who you are, you will begin to fulfill the purpose for which you were created.

8. Insecurity is often a result of insufficient provision, education, or emotional stability during childhood.

9. Healing from insecurity begins the moment we acknowledge our insufficiencies and begin to allow others to mend our broken places.

10. The more certain we are of who God created us to be, the less tolerant we will be of those who presume to wrongly define us.

Words of Wisdom

Now faith is the assurance of things hoped for, the conviction of things not seen.

—HEBREWS 11:1

Power Quote

The best way to predict the future is to create it.

—PETER F. DRUCKER

Plan of Action

The more certain we are of who God created us to be, the less tolerant we will be of those who wrongly define us. Be willing and assertive in your desire to build and finish the assignment God has given you. Work on seeing yourself through the eyes of your magnificent Creator. Renew your self-image. Create a list of all the dreams you long to fulfill. Refuse to become a victim of your circumstances. Know who you are and accomplish every dream.

Conclusion

In a world filled with choices, chaos, and drama, it is reassuring to realize our lives are not dangling mercilessly over the cliffs of uncertainty. In fact, we should take great comfort in knowing we can live our lives with purpose and intention. Within our reach are golden opportunities to embrace grace and pursue a fulfilling life.

Today I celebrate the passionate few who have courageously picked up the pieces of their shattered lives. I applaud their tenacity and resolve to live life to the fullest. I praise their drive to refuse failure while reaching for success. Believe me, I understand that conquering fear and overcoming dysfunctional behavior is no easy feat. I recognize the monumental effort it takes to transform heartache into a beautiful montage of grace and goodness.

When I think about courageous people, I am reminded of my friend Caroline, who for a solid year worked through painful memories to emerge victorious, free from the chains of rejection and low self-esteem. No longer weighed down by the negative opinions of verbal abusers or manipulators, Caroline now embraces life with renewed confidence and self-assurance. Was the journey easy? No; many times it was painful. The voyage toward wholeness proved challenging for her and those she relied upon for support and encouragement. The truth is, the road to wholeness is filled with bumps, hurdles, and unexpected trials. While I cannot guarantee a journey full of comfort and ease, I can promise you that with the right attitude and God-centered plan it can be a successful one.

Right now, I pray for you who are journeying down the road of recovery. How I wish I were able to hear your story, to sit and share a meal, to talk you through the process or walk this path with you. While many of us may never meet in person, I believe this book is the starting point of a lifelong friendship. My goal throughout our journey has been to renew how you think and respond to rejection. To assist you in reversing the negative effects of rejection while teaching you to embrace rejection as a positive, life-altering encounter. At the onset of reading this book I am sure your focus was fixed squarely on the negative aspects of rejection—in particular, how up until this point rejection had robbed you of relationships, security, and opportunities. Prayerfully, your perception of rejection has been altered.

Of the six billion people on the earth today, I dare say few know how to effectively deal with rejection. For the most part, rejection continues to consume their passion for life and eats away at their waning self-esteem. Their encounters with rejection have been sheer devastation. The result is, they avoid rejection at all costs. It is my sincere desire they learn to see rejection in a positive light, eventually embracing rejection as a positive part of their self-portrait.

If you read the principles in this book carefully, you will wholeheartedly attest there is an upside to rejection. You clearly see rejection as a hidden, if not golden, opportunity and are now ready to embrace the many benefits of rejection. In fact, I want you to treat rejection as a valuable friend. A friend who reveals secrets, alerts you to danger, exposes poor relationship choices, and motivates you to make wise decisions. Remember, rejection is unavoidable. Your reaction to rejection determines how it responds to you. Treat rejection like an enemy and it will respond accordingly. Treat rejection like an invisible bodyguard and it will protect, guide, and maneuver you through a world of hidden danger.

> Rejection is unavoidable. Your reaction to rejection determines how it responds to you.

As we now move forward, I want to thank you for your willingness to allow God's Word to change your perception of rejection. I appreciate your enthusiasm for opening your heart to the goodness of God's love and your mind to the powerful precepts of His wisdom. I will think and pray for you with great affection.

> May grace and peace be yours in abundance in the knowledge of God and of Jesus our Lord.
>
> —2 Peter 1:2

Notes

Chapter 2

1. Louise Hay, "Key Principles," *The Healing Project*, last modified March 19, 2010, accessed July 19, 2012, http://healingprojectsite .com/principles/.
2. Tamara Baruhovich, "Self-Talk: How You Communicate," *Tools for Abundance*, last modified June 7, 2012, accessed July 19, 2012, http://www.tools-for-abundance.com/self-talk.html.

Chapter 3

1. "Types of Fear," DealingWithFear.org, last modified 2007, accessed July 19, 2012, http://www.dealingwithfear.org/types-of-fear.htm.

Chapter 5

1. Merriam-Webster.com, s.v. "ability," accessed October 14, 2012, http://www.merriam-webster.com/dictionary/ability.
2. Ibid., s.v. "capacity," accessed October 12, 2012, http://www.merriam-webster.com/dictionary/capacity.
3. Joan E. Grusec, "Parent's Attitudes and Beliefs: Their Impact on Children's Development," in *Encyclopedia on Early Childhood Development* (Toronto, Canada: Centre of Excellence for Early Childhood Development, 2006), [[#]].
4. Merriam-Webster.com, s.v. "friend," accessed October 12, 2012, http://www.merriam-webster.com/dictionary/friend.

Chapter 6

1. Merriam-Webster.com, s.v. "helicopter parent," accessed July 16, 2012, http://www.merriam-webster.com/dictionary/helicopterparent.
2. Gaither, Gloria. *What My Parents Did Right* (Carol Stream, IL: Tyndale House Publishers, 1994).

Chapter 7

1. Dave McNeff, "It Only has 40,000 Miles," Sermon Logos, last modified October 2009, accessed July 21, 2012, http://sermons.logos.com/submissions/108625-It-Only-Has-40-000-Miles.
2. TheFreeDictionary.com, s.v. "web," accessed July 16, 2012, http://www.thefreedictionary.com/web.

Chapter 9

1. "But They Did Not Give Up," Emory University, last modified 2012, accessed July 22, 2012, http://www.des.emory.edu/mfp/efficacynotgiveup.html.
2. Geoffrey Brewer, "Snakes Top List of Americans' Fears," Gallup Poll, last modified March 19, 2001, accessed July 22, 2012, http://www.gallup.com/poll/1891/Snakes-Top-List-Americans-Fears.aspx.
3. TheFreeDictionary.com, s.v. "emotion," accessed October 15, 2012, http://www.thefreedictionary.com/emotion.
4. Dictionary.com, s.v. "detoxification," accessed October 15, 2012, http://dictionary.reference.com/browse/detox?s=t.

Chapter 10

1. Marianne Williamson, *Return to Love* (New York: Harper Collins, 1992), 190–91.

Acknowledgments

This work is the result of a lifetime of learning and personal development. It is a composite of the love and wisdom lavishly bestowed by my mentors, supporters, friends, and family. I remain in awe of your many acts of kindness and the investment of time, energy, wisdom, and support. Words of gratitude would fail to express how thankful my heart is that we have made this journey together.

I would like to thank the staff of Thomas Nelson Publishers for believing in me and for breathing life into this work. A special thank-you to Joel Miller for being the first to catch the vision for this book and overseeing it to completion. To Kristin Parrish, my superb editor, your relentless pursuit of excellence was a tremendous source of encouragement.

To Robby, my best friend and partner in life, thank you for being unwavering in an ever-changing world. To our children and extended family, thank you for your patience and grace.

ACKNOWLEDGMENTS

To my friend Charlotte Hansen, who helped with the early stages of this work, you are sheer inspiration and a true monarch.

To all the fabulous women of the Christian Women in Media Association (CWIMA), who encourage, uplift, and inspire new chapters in each other's lives.

About the Author

As one of the nation's leading conference speakers, Tracey travels more than forty weeks a year, sharing biblical principles and wisdom with diverse audiences throughout America. Tracey's real-life experiences—though painful and challenging—have enabled her to identify with the hurting, lonely, and rejected. Whether speaking to men, women CEOs, or the homeless, Tracey's love and passion for rewriting the lives of the brokenhearted make her messages relevant and empowering.

As a life coach and mentorship founder of The Winning Woman, Tracey's heart is to see lives changed, hearts healed, and dreams fulfilled. Her heart is transparent, and her message is simple: "Your life can change—you can change!"

Passionate about reaching people with the gospel message, Tracey is a frequent guest on national television programs and is the host of *Today with Tracey*, which reaches millions via satellite, cable television, and the Internet. She is an advocate for those who have experienced rejection, poverty, or emotional abuse. Having conquered great pain by applying biblical principles, she ministers the message of truth to those searching for wholeness and redemption.

Tracey was awarded an honorary doctorate in divinity degree in 2006 and was presented with the Dallas Exceptional Service Award in 2008 by Women in Christian Media. She serves on the advisory board for the Christian Women in Media Association (CWIMA), a non profit organization, advancing Christian women who influence culture through media.